D1218375

Demystifying Parole

Demystifying Parole

Janet Schmidt
San Diego State University

Lexington Books
D.C. Heath and Company
Lexington, Massachusetts
Toronto

Library of Congress Cataloging in Publication Data

Schmidt, Janet.
   Demystifying parole.

   Includes bibliographical references and index.
   1. Parole—United States. 2. United States. Board of Parole. I. Title.
HV9304.S34   364.6'2'0973   76-48375
ISBN 0-669-01145-2

Published simultaneously in Canada.

Printed in the United States of America.

International Standard Book Number: 0-669-01145-2

Library of Congress Catalog Card Number: 76-48375

To the revolutionary struggles of working people, inside and outside the prisons; to teachers and friends who have shared their knowledge and time with me; to Heidi and the future.

Contents

List of Figures and Tables

Preface

The process of paroling inmates from prison institutions has never been clearly revealed or understood. Parole has appeared to be a process of selecting for release those prison inmates considered good risks regarding their potential for recidivism. However, much more is involved than predicting success in remaining out of prison. This book attempts to explore some of these other elements, as well as analyze the way in which social science has been used to serve the interests and needs of a political administrative body rather than to provide an accurate conceptualization of the function and practice of a social institution.

Parole boards have been under attack from various sources because they have operated in a capricious and arbitrary manner, with total discretion to parole or deny at will. The actual procedures under which parole boards operate have been a secret. Taking the activities of the U.S. Board of Parole as exemplary of how parole boards function, the following investigation attempts to penetrate the boundaries of parole board discretion to analyze the practice of deciding to parole or deny. Several methods have been used in this task: individual case study, statistical empiricism, and political economy.

Acknowledgments

I wish to acknowledge the major contributions made by Ricardo Klorman in organizing and analyzing the data used in this study. I also wish to thank Bill Hodge for his organizational help, and the Campus Computer Network of UCLA for the use of its facilities.

I am grateful for the assistance of Nasatir, Sherman and Hirsch, attorneys-at-law, in making available to me its files and experience in dealing with the U.S. Board of Parole. I especially thank Victor Sherman, whose insights and help were invaluable.

I am most grateful to John Horton, whose classes provided me with a fundamental basis for understanding complex social issues. As for my students, hopefully I can make some small contribution to the growth of their revolutionary consciousness.

Introduction:
To Parole or Deny

The theory and practice of parole has been an integral part of the penal system in the United States since incarceration rather than execution became the ultimate form of repressive state control. Once men became inmates and went into penitentiaries, procedures had to be devised for processing them out. The state had to make room for ever-growing numbers and new generations of "criminals." The ideology and practice of parole was developed, whereby the carrot of release could be held up for all, and yet control exercised to sift through the inmate population and select only those who were sufficiently "reformed" so as not to cause any more trouble for the existing order. Those who were felt to be a threat could be warehoused indefinitely. This selection process and the federal agency created to organize and manage it are the focus of this research.

Many criminologists have investigated parole, primarily with the aim of aiding the parole board in its task. The administrative problems of parole boards were seen as problems for criminologists. The bulk of their research focused on "prediction," and asked the question, "Is the parole board using the right factors for selection?" Under the theoretical sway of positivism,[1] the majority of researchers sought to quantify and objectify a relationship between information about the inmates and any later law-abiding behavior. The problem was seen as one of having to identify features about an individual that correlated with his or her ability to stay out of prison, expressed in terms of a prediction of "risk." The focus was on the individual's psychological makeup or immediate social environment, and not on the social order itself. These criminologists dealt in abstract and static categories. They created typologies of "social types" according to categories such as "ne'er do well" and "socially inadequate," and then attempted to determine for the parole boards what these "types" would do once paroled.[2] The issue of parole was not seen as a political issue, but, rather, one of value-free science attempting to improve technique. Dimensions of power involved in social relationships were not discussed. Researchers shared the values and social worlds of the board members, and no thought was given to alternative perceptions and interpretations. An underlying essential social consensus was assumed, as was a pluralist conception of the organization of political power.

Traditional criminologists have been unable to rid themselves of ideological, common-sense understandings about the nature of prison and parole. They have aided the powerful to control the powerless. They have spewed forth a morass of ideology that supports existing ways of conceptualizing and dealing with prison populations. Ignoring structural elements and distributions of power, they have maintained a static and narrow focus on isolated, "improperly socialized" individuals. Prisoners have been defined as passive victims of psychological or social forces of which they are unaware or from which they are unable to break away. They have not been seen as active agents, responding politically to situations engendered by the structural and material conditions of their existence.[3]

Criminologists who have done research in parole prediction have provided the board with an unending source of mystification around which they can mobilize and encourage the spending of thousands of dollars, years of time, and the production of volumes of paperwork. For example, the major accomplishment of one of the most well-known studies of "corrections" in the United States was indicated by the author to be "the stimulation of much more research in correctional agencies."[4] We can also illustrate this phenomenon by a statement from a criminologist who was involved in a recent study of the parole decision-making process:

First, we need to ascertain whether the use of predictive data does, indeed, improve decision-making. If so, in what respects and to what extent? This is an obvious question, but the methodology for answering it may be difficult and certainly will take time.

Second, how can we improve the model we produce? We do know that until correctional systems can produce records which deal with experience more accurately than is now the case, the more sophisticated statistical methods which are available will be of no use in improving predictions or feedback.

Third, how can a parole board organize itself to make good use of feedback? It is one thing to pronounce the desirability of modifying policy in terms of experience, but quite another to develop procedures for doing so.[5]

We are left feeling overwhelmed in the face of all that needs to be done. While the carrot of ultimate success through "science" is held out, caution as to whether a solution ever can be achieved is the major thrust of the argument. Thus, the status quo is upheld, jobs are maintained, power is preserved, and criticism is contained. The board and its "scientists" are "working on it." It is a problem that will never be solved, however, for it is conceived of in the wrong terms.

Researchers themselves sum up the value of their expensive research:

Is the development of prediction methods as important as it has been thought to be? Our answer on this issue is a qualified one: prediction methods are useful, but mainly as a research tool. In assisting in the decision-making processes of parole discretion, prediction is one element only and its relevance involves a value judgment.[6]

What, then, are the correct questions to ask? Rather than conceptualize the problem in the traditional fragmented way, in terms of deciding whether statistical predictive devices aid in determining who will "succeed" and who will "fail" on parole, this research begins with an analysis of the specific theory and practice of parole, past and present, attempting to shed any preconceived notions as to what the process is all about. This theory and practice are then related to the historical and material conditions within which parole boards operate. Parole cannot be understood in a vacuum. It is part of both ideological argument and concrete method of processing people through an institutional system of social relations. It is a very important part of the mystification surrounding imprisonment, so we must begin to ask what is the reality of parole.

The first chapter provides historical background regarding the development of ideology and practice relating to parole. The policies and procedures of the U.S. Board of Parole are examined as an illustrative example of the structure and operation of parole today.

Chapter 2 is a discussion of the case of the *United States of America* vs. *David Donner*, which illustrates the board's actual practice in the decision-making process.[a] From an analysis of the experience of David Donner, many of the specific concerns and factors the board considers important in making its determination of release or further incarceration become apparent. The issues that emerge from an investigation of this case point out the same contradictions as those involved in current controversies surrounding the board. Studying a particular case provides insight into the actual operation of an institution and raises many important questions that can be pursued through other methods. This is especially true of the parole board, whose methods of operation and policies are relatively unknown and secret because of their great discretionary power. Although analysis of a specific case enables us to discern important characteristics about an institution, there are limits as to the generalizations and predictions that can be made based upon it. Therefore, to investigate further the policies and procedures of parole, the extended study described in Chapter 3 was undertaken.

Chapter 3 consists of an empirical investigation of the parole board's decision-making process, using the method of multivariate nominal analysis. In this study, data used were gathered by the National Council on Crime and Delinquency on 7,286 inmates in federal prisons who appeared before the U.S. Board of Parole between 1970 and 1972. The data were gathered in collaboration with the U.S. Board of Parole under a grant from the National Institute of Law Enforcement and Criminal Justice of the Law Enforcement Assistance Administration. The population from which this sample was chosen included all cases considered for parole during that period. The data consisted of information regarding the background characteristics and past and present performance of these potential parolees. The problem to be investigated was whether factors claimed by the board in various statements and lists of criteria to be those they considered in making a determination, actually had some power in explaining their decisions.

Multivariate nominal analysis generates several statistics that indicate the amount of variance on the dependent variable (here parole decision), which is

---

[a] The names of defendants and codefendants that are discussed are fictitious; however, the cases and events are factual.

explained by the independent predictor variables (here the background characteristics of inmates). Results indicate there is some disparity between what the board says it has been considering in its paroling policy and what factors seem to have an effect on the outcome of parole hearings. The generalized R^2 indicates that two-thirds of the variance remains unexplained by the 27 predictor variables we have used. It appears that insofar as overall effect on the parole decision is concerned, length of sentence and amount of time served are the most valuable predictors of parole-decision outcome, and these are determined from a judgment about the severity of the offense, rather than rehabilitation, prediction of success on parole, future plans, or other criteria the board says it considers.

The fourth chapter contains a theoretical analysis of criminological research in parole. Of particular interest is how social science has been used for political purposes to produce ideology that supports existing structures and power relationships. Interrelated with this discussion is an analysis of the three elements of the new parole board guidelines for decision making: (1) parole prognosis or "prediction," (2) offense severity, and (3) amount of time to be served. These guidelines are the latest statement by the parole board about what its criteria are. A final concern of this chapter is a discussion of the class nature of prison and parole from the perspective of dialectical materialism[7] or political economy. Traditional criminologists have not recognized the fact that inmates come primarily from the same low social class and form an important part of the marginal surplus population or industrial reserve army of labor. A very small percentage of individuals in prison are inherently "dangerous" or mentally unbalanced; yet, this small percentage is used to justify the imprisonment of thousands, primarily the poor who are there because of their position in the social structure. There is an important relationship that must be recognized between "criminals" and workers, and a link between crime and unemployment that will be investigated. It has been suggested that to prevent minority, radical, and working-class movements from collaborating and gaining strength, they have been criminalized.

a drop of water
  tasting salty
    upon your lips
      after—
          leaving a
            trail
                upon your cheek

days pass
  the taste
  still upon your lips—

then—
    the salt water
      vanishes
    bitterness
      the new taste—

—finally no taste—

but feeling—
    inescapable
    —you can't lose it
or let it out—

No one knows
  —but you—
    the anguish—
pent up
    within—
        your mind
          your body
            your heart

feeling also
  vanishes
    there is
              nothing—

are you
    still alive?

Patricia S. Strauss

1

Theory and Practice of Parole

Day after day, day after day,
We stuck, nor breath, nor motion;
As idle as a painted ship
Upon a painted ocean.

Samuel Taylor Coleridge

Behind prison walls is a world that revolves around *time*. On the mind of every prisoner is the day he or she will finally be released. There are just a few ways by which an individual will leave prison: (1) after serving his full sentence; (2) after serving his sentence minus "good time"[1] (*mandatory release*); (3) after serving one-third of his sentence or a court-imposed minimum time, thereby becoming eligible for parole;[2] (4) after being pardoned by the chief executive; (5) by dying; or (6) by escaping. Obviously, being paroled is the primary concern of a prisoner.[3]

This chapter investigates the historical background of the parole process and the theoretical premises upon which it developed as an integral part of the penal system. It also examines the structure and operation of parole today, using the policies and procedures of the U.S. Board of Parole as an illustrative example.

Classical and Positivist Ideology

The penal system can only be understood in relation to the dominant modes of economic production and reproduction of social relations. As European societies underwent changes from feudal to capitalistic social and economic forms during the sixteenth to nineteenth centuries, there developed philosophies and ideologies[4] to explain and support the new system. Emphasis was placed on the "rights of man." These had to be defined and protected, for freedom against feudal interference and new individual initiative were essential for early capitalist development. In this context the "classical" view of crime, as delineated in criminological theory, emerged:[5] men came together to create freely a civil society to prevent a war of all against all and to protect their personal property and welfare. The function of legal punishment was to ensure the continued existence of society. Lawbreaking was characterized as irrational or pathological, a result of personal inadequacies. Men had a free choice whether or not to break

1

the law. Classical theorists concentrated on the law and the administration of control, primarily to build an ideological and structural framework for protection from the feudal nobility. However, contradictions in the classical scheme soon became apparent, for criminal "irrationality" was concentrated among the propertyless who did not always have "free choice" in fulfilling the social contract. Modifications in the classical scheme occurred as it became necessary to recognize some of the social processes involved in human activity. Men were still held accountable for their actions, but their past history and present situation were taken into account in that they would affect a person's likelihood of being reformed. Some structures were seen as more conducive to free choice and the making of correct moral decisions. This modified classical model forms the basis of most legal and penal systems.

In the nineteenth century, as capitalist relationships were solidifying, the "positivist" school of thought emerged. Ideological changes correspond to political and economic changes. Positivism emerged as competitive capitalism began giving way to monopoly capitalism. In the face of new corporate realities, the competitive individual was no longer a viable force. Positivism called for the replacement of the free-will doctrine with emphasis on the deterministic nature of human action and insistence on "scientific method" as the means of finding out what the natural, absolute, and eternal laws of human existence were.[6] The criminal was propelled by forces beyond his awareness; it was the job of the scientific expert to unearth and explain these forces to him. The criminal was an irrational, insufficiently socialized person, and greater control was necessary to correct his deficiencies. There was no suggestion that perhaps an alternative, authentic morality and rationality were involved in response to material conditions and class circumstances. Whereas for the classicists, the individual was an active element in the social process, for the positivists, the individual was a passive pawn of external forces.

Classical ideas of free will came to be part of the "conservative" outlook; positivist ideas of determinism became part of "liberalism." These views are not entirely antagonistic, however, for both recognize ultimate individual responsibility, both assume that a fundamental consensus exists as to the "needs" of "society," and both look for means of effective social control. The social and behavioral sciences carried on their studies of crime within the positivist frame of reference, while legal and penal practice continued to be based on the classical model. The positivists shifted the focus of study from the law to the criminal actor. They sought to develop quantitative ways of distinguishing "criminal" from "normal" behavior, based on the assumption that a consensus existed about what normal behavior was and that law was a freely entered into contract crystallizing that agreement. For them, the problem was that social control was breaking down because it was not scientific or efficient enough.[7] Through the development of new technology, society would be saved. The positivists' great success was in separating the study of crime from study of the state. Attention was focused on the psychological and situational reasons why an individual failed to internalize norms agreed upon by the majority as being for the common good. Ignored by both classical and positivist schemes was the fact that meaning is class structured and that the power to define morality, legality, and criminality lay in the hands of those who exercised hegemony.

The development of penal concepts such as parole illustrates the way in which practice that was functional for the capitalist state was legitimated by emerging theories. As positivist thought and method became dominant, issues revolving around parole centered on the individual criminal and ways in which he could be treated, reformed, resocialized, and sent home to his appropriate place.

Origins of Parole

Parole has been defined as "a treatment program in which an offender, after serving part of a term in a correctional institution, is conditionally released, under supervision and treatment by a parole worker."[8] The word "parole" comes from the French, meaning "promise" or "word of honor." To understand some of the ideas and assumptions on which parole is based, it is necessary to take a look at English seventeenth- and eighteenth-century policy regarding convicted felons. In England's colonies there was a great shortage of cheap labor, and the search for workers became a pressing problem. Workers were needed in the mother country, so the government decided to grant stays of execution to prisoners who would agree to be shipped abroad to work until the end of their imposed sentence. Deportation to America involved forgiving part of an inmate's sentence and placing him in a free community as an indentured servant. However, the slave trade put an end to the labor shortage in the American colonies and made deportation there unprofitable. Also, convict labor could not exist alongside free labor the moment the latter assumed appreciable size. The cheap labor of prisoners and the existence of a large labor supply was opposed to the interests of free laborers in maintaining high wages for themselves. Political conditions finally put an end to transportation to America.

However, it was impossible to accommodate the increasing number of criminals in the existing dilapidated prisons in England at a time when the labor market was oversupplied. It was necessary to eliminate from the mother country people who were considered dangerous to society. After the American colonies revolted, convicts were sent to Australia to help exploit the land. However, these later deportees did not become indentured servants but, rather, remained under the control of the government. They were occupied primarily on government projects, but at the end of the official workday could hire themselves out to private employers for wages. Those whose work and conduct were good could have their sentences remitted and receive a grant of land and a *ticket of leave*.

This was a declaration signed by the colonial governor excusing a convict from further government work and allowing him to live independently but within a particular district. In the middle of the nineteenth century, the structure of the "ticket-of-leave" system was further clarified. For good behavior a prisoner could earn a certain number of "marks" a week, which would cut down his period of confinement. For misbehavior, his marks were taken away.

The ticket of leave came into use in England as part of the penal system, and a further dimension was added: supervision of those released. In the United States, similar measures were instituted. Inmates had been difficult to control; it was felt that if there were a system whereby prisoners knew that if they were good or bad it would make a difference in the time served in prison, more of them would opt for being "good." Thus, a system of parole was introduced as a means by which behavior might be modified and controlled, which ostensibly placed responsibility for reduction of confinement upon the prisoner himself. In parole we find the basic concept of *indeterminancy*: the prisoner is told he will be released early if he measures up to some set standard.

The Indeterminate Sentence

To understand parole, it is necessary to understand the indeterminate sentence. The fact that all prisoners will come before a parole board that will determine whether rehabilitation has been reached and the individual has achieved "parole readiness" means that all sentences are in effect indeterminate. Parole is the dominant method of release; for every ten men who leave prison, nine do so by parole.[9]

The indeterminate sentence was a further step in increasing control over prisoners. It is integrally related to the "medical model" and the expressed aim of "treatment" and "rehabilitation." The *medical model* assumes that there is something wrong with an individual that needs to be corrected for him to be able to adapt to the existing social order. That order itself is not questioned. The *medical model of physical disease* refers to processes independent of the social order. The *medical model of criminality*, however, is based upon understandings constructed within particular social conditions, and can never be free of these relationships.

The idea of the criminal as sick originated in the nineteenth century, with the ideas of determinism replacing those of free will. If an individual's behavior was caused by social or psychological forces outside of his consciousness and control, help was required to provide him with the understanding and guidance he could not achieve himself. Correction by experts was necessary. If an individual was sick, how could the authorities know before treatment began how long it would take to cure him? It was necessary, to be consistent with the ideology of treatment, to initiate sentences of an indeterminate time range within which an individual could be "cured." Thus, much of the sentencing responsibility of judges was transferred to parole boards. The indeterminate sentence was applauded by both conservatives and liberals. For conservatives it promised the possibility of greater control, legitimated in psychological principles. For liberals it held out humanitarian aims through the individualization of sentences and the prospect of social betterment through increasingly rational "scientific" means. The indeterminate sentence offered the potential for a quick solution to crime and overcrowded prisons through earlier release of criminals who had been treated and reformed. The problem was seen as one of changing individual behavior. The ideology of treatment was also a way of further legitimating the penal process and securing the cooperation of prisoners themselves in seeming to offer them a way to improve their lot. Institutions would become the laboratory for social improvement, much as the educational ideology claimed the schools would become.

The rationales supporting the indeterminate sentence came out around the turn of the century. At this time capitalist expansion had resulted in the accumulation of wealth and power by a few businessmen, and had on the other hand created a large class of persons (the "dangerous classes") who were thrown into conditions of owning nothing. It became necessary to further manage these groups of people and stem their potential for revolt. This is not necessarily best handled through repressive measures, but through the power of rhetoric and ideology, concealing the true nature of the social processes involved beneath the level of appearances. Therefore, it is not surprising that the *new penology* (treatment rather than custody) emerged only in rhetoric and not in practice.[10] Control was still the major issue, and "treatment" a new ideological weapon for continuation of the status quo. (Thus, today when criminologists say that treatment has failed, they ignore the fact that rehabilitation was primarily an ideological tool and never a principal practice of prison institutions.)

Underlying the practice of parole is the assumption that inmates can be classified into a limited number of diagnostic categories and that an appropriate treatment program can be designed. It is also assumed that prisons create an environment where treatment can take place. Another fundamental premise is that there is a need for continuing evaluation of an inmate's program to determine some optimum time for release, and that the parole board is capable of judging when this has been reached. It is also assumed that some persons are unsafe to release, that their crime was so heinous, or that they are totally beyond reforming. Periodic checks must be made, therefore, to ensure that even if some point of readiness is reached, those who are "still too dangerous" may be retained in prison. What happens in practice is that a charade develops between the board and inmates, who must devise strategies designed to show those with evaluative power that they are "ready."[11] This is difficult because statutory criteria regarding when an inmate may be paroled are so broad and general as to be useless, and the board's actual criteria have been, in effect, a mystery.[12]

During the recent Hearings on Parole in 1972 before the House of Representatives Committee on the Judiciary, Professor Leonard Orland of the University of Connecticut Law School pointed out what the indeterminate sentence means: "He who commits a crime shall be imprisoned until the parole board decides to let him out."[13]

It is difficult not to recognize the element of coercion in the ideal of rehabilitation. It is always the powerful who attempt to change the powerless who threaten existing conditions and refuse to assume particular roles within the system. That "treatment" is supposed to take place in a prison situation is obviously an antagonistic contradiction that cannot be resolved. In prison, control is the primary motive. There are many prisoners and few guards. Routine and rules are of great importance to maintain stability. People are held in prison against their will. The reality of prisoners' lives has been different from that of their captors.

It is easy to understand how the ideology of treatment has led to greater use of "behavior modification" techniques within prisons,[14] including psycho-surgery for "violent" individuals, pills and tranquilizers for uncooperative inmates, and more sophisticated manipulation of rewards and punishments, all in the name of treatment through value-free scientific means. In the concluding chapter of this study, we investigate this issue of research as political and ideological and not "scientific." For now, to illustrate and illuminate the preceding discussion, we investigate a specific parole agency, the U.S. Board of Parole. Through a detailed analysis of its structure and operation, we can see the ideologies surrounding the "criminal justice" system in concrete form.

Creation of the U.S. Board of Parole

The U.S. Board of Parole was created by Congress in 1930. Before then, under a law enacted in 1910, each federal prison had its own parole board, comprised of the warden, medical officer, and superintendent of prisons in the Department of Justice, Washington, D.C. Their tasks included the parole decision and parole supervision in the community afterwards. These boards would recommend parole and the attorney general would make the final decision. In 1930, when the separate prison boards were merged into one board consisting of three members, no substantive changes were made in the methods by which decisions were to be made or in the conditions under which United States prisoners would be paroled. What occurred was merely a transfer of power to a centralized authority with no tasks other than parole decision making and supervision.

In December 1929 hearings were held before the Committee on the Judiciary of the House of Representatives.[15] Discussion of the "prison problem" was of primary concern. Six bills relating to prisons were before the House, including the construction of new and larger jails and penitentiaries, provision for the employment of prisoners (with the specific intent to "diversify employment so as not to concentrate competition with free labor and industry in any one line of work"),[16] reorganization of the Bureau of Prisons and increase of its personnel, and the reorganization of the system of parole under one centralized administrative board. The attorney general testified before the House that federal prisons had become overcrowded and were full to more than double their capacity.[17] He also pointed out that there were "riots" in penitentiaries all over the country. It was therefore necessary to do some rethinking and reorganizing of penal institutions and the administrative bodies dealing with them. In discussing the bills before the House, one of the committee members raised the question of whether the attorney general would recommend the repeal of any laws that had caused the congested condition in the prisons. This was dismissed by the chairman and the attorney general as not germane to the discussion.[18] They did not wish to discuss the laws but, rather, the offenders. Debate was to remain centered around the administrative task of implementing the new bills, in a context totally ignoring the larger issues involved. The problems were defined in abstract terms of providing for humanitarian treatment of prisoners, correcting the idleness of prisoners, reducing expense of crime control to the taxpayers, and finding some sort of employment for prisoners to rehabilitate them and make use of their potential labor power. ("The idle man is the devil's workshop.")[19] The issue of parole is contained in the real issue of the increase of the federal prison population, which had grown at the rate of 10 percent a year from 1919 to 1929.[20] Requests for parole had increased from 600 to 9,000 a year.

It was pointed out in the discussions that $9,000,000 a year had been spent by the superintendent of prisons in travelling to various penitentiaries for parole meetings with wardens and medical officers. At one meeting there had been 1,014 applications for parole. Out of these, 750 men had been seen in a three-day period, at approximately three to five minutes a case. It was obviously becoming necessary to have a group that did nothing but pass judgment on parole.

There was never any question of changing the substantive institutionalized methods of operation within the penal system, or any real rethinking of imprisonment itself. Rather, the problem was how to continue to implement the same policies. The problem of maintaining the system of parole was resolved through creation of the U.S. Board of Parole.

Structure, Rules, Policies, and Procedures of the
U.S. Board of Parole

The U.S. Board of Parole is an autonomous body that is part of the Department of Justice and subject to the attorney general for administrative purposes. The board's headquarters are in Washington, D.C. Supporting its activities are a staff director, legal counsel, parole and youth division executives, and a small clerical staff. The board is aided by personnel in the various penal institutions and by the United States probation officers attached to the various federal district courts, who also act as parole agents. The Board of Parole consisted of eight members appointed by the president with the advice and consent of the Senate, serving staggered six-year terms.[21] Five members specialized in adult cases and three in the Youth Correction Division. All members vote on controversial cases or those referred for *en banc* consideration (all members present).

By law these eight members are not required to have any particular background or training or be members of any political parties. The membership of the board consists "primarily of those employed in the professional correctional field or in related professions dealing with human behavior."[22] Of the eight members in 1970, five had a background in the field of "corrections." The others included a newspaper journalist (the one female member), a principal and superintendent of public schools, and a lawyer who served as a law specialist for the U.S. Navy and other governmental agencies. Some of the members were reappointments and had served previous terms on the board. All of the members had worked in one capacity or another for a governmental agency. Only one member had had training in a field of the social or behavioral sciences.

Because of increasingly large case loads, in 1970 the board increased its staff by the addition of eight hearing examiners who conducted a majority of the hearings at the various penitentiaries while the eight members remained at headquarters in Washington. Hearing examiners made recommendations regarding parole or denial, and board members made the final decisions. In June 1974 the board reorganized itself again into various regional areas of the country.[23] Five board members became regional directors, and three remained in Washington as the National Appellate Board. Authority was granted to hearing examiners to make decisions, as long as these were within specific guidelines that had been newly created. If decisions were outside these guidelines, review and modification would be made by regional directors and/or the board in Washington. The fact that the board was the target of heavy criticism from the legal profession, the press, the American Civil Liberties Union (ACLU), members of Congress, and various individuals led to the need to delegate authority to give the semblance of accomplishing at least some of the reforms being sought. However, the board still wished to retain its power. The development of the guidelines would ensure that they would. "Obviously decision guidelines of the type developed could enable the Board to more effectively exercise control over the decisions of the expanded and decentralized staff proposed."[24]

Parole hearings are conducted by a panel of two hearing examiners, who must concur on a decision. If there is disagreement, the regional administrative hearing examiner casts the deciding vote. The board has estimated that the first two persons disagree on about 30 percent of the decisions.[25] If the decision is outside the guidelines, and the administrative hearing examiner does not concur, the decision must be reviewed by the regional director and the Appellate Board in Washington.

A hearing generally lasts about ten minutes.[26] Within this short time the board is supposed to decide whether an inmate is "cured." George Reed, former chairman of the U.S. Board of Parole, indicated that parole boards are "attempting to evaluate personality modification, if any, toward rehabilitation of the individual."[27] The information they have to base their decisions on comes entirely from the prison staff. According to the new rules, a prisoner is to be informed of the decision within 15 working days of the date of the hearing. Previous to this, it sometimes took from one to three months for an inmate to be so informed.

Federal statutes authorize the board to release prisoners on parole, set the conditions of parole, and revoke parole for violation of those conditions (18 U.S.C. 4203). When making a determination, the board has three alternatives: an inmate may be paroled, continued to a fixed date some time in the future for another hearing, or denied parole and continued to the date his sentence expires minus "good time." The statutory criteria for release of a prisoner on parole are extremely broad: (1) if, in the opinion of the board, such release is not incompatible with the welfare of society; (2) if the inmate has observed substantially the roles of the institution in which he is confined; and (3) if there is a reasonable probability that he will live and remain at liberty without violating the laws.[28] One of the major criticisms of the board, even as late as 1969, has been that it never announced rules, standards, or guidelines to interpret the generalities of the statute, or even publicly announced the criteria that are considered.[29] Since the board was designed to make decisions whether or not to parole, the criteria used are of the utmost importance.

In 1972 the board made 18,944 decisions. It granted 6,174 paroles (37.1%), continued 4,216 to completion of their full sentence (25.3%), and continued 6,250 (37.6%) for further review. In providing statistical clarification of its practice, the board has indicated that it only considers final decisions, ignoring the 6,250 inmates who were placed in *limbo* (continued for further review). The board prefers to conclude that it grants parole in 50 percent of its cases.[30] A false impression is given. Tables 1-1 and 1-2 indicate the board's statistical manipulations.

As mentioned earlier, the U.S. Board of Parole has been under attack for various reasons. The principle charge leveled against it is that it operates in a capricious and arbitrary manner. Parole board decisions are not subject to judicial review or appeal to any outside agency.[31] The actual procedures under which the board operates have been and still are a secret. The board specifically points out that it is not subject to the provisions of the Administrative Procedure Act (5 U.S.C. 553 [b]), which governs administrative agencies of the United States government.[32] Inmates who appear before the board are not

Table 1-1
Work Load of the Board, 1972

Type of Decision	Number
Parole and reparole	6,174[a]
Continue to expiration	4,216
Continue for further review	6,250
	16,640[b]

Source: U.S. Board of Parole, *Biennial Report*, 1970-1972.
[a]4,275 adults.
[b]2,304 additional decisions were made to revoke, reinstate, or review particular cases.

Table 1-2
Number and Percentage of Adult Prisoners Paroled, Final Decisions Only, 1972

Year	Decisions	Continued to Expiration	Paroled	Percent Paroled
1972	8,253	4,127	4,126[a]	50.0

Source: U.S. Board of Parole, *Biennial Report*, 1970-1972.
[a]Does not include reparoles. (It is unclear why the number of persons continued to expiration does not match in the two tables.)

entitled to be represented by counsel in an adversary proceeding.[33] Inmates are not allowed to see reports and documents being used in the decision-making process or to see the hearing examiner's summary and recommendations. Rules of evidence do not apply in the hearing, such as whether the board may consider illegally seized evidence or the crime for which the individual was arrested rather than the crime for which he was convicted. Most of the criticism has been directed towards reform through clarification of the specific criteria used by the board in its decision-making capacity. This has been called *structuring discretion* and is intended to provide for fair and equitable treatment of prisoners, more rational and effective prison-release procedures, and clearly articulated policies for greater consistency of operation. One other area of reform that has taken place revolves around the issue of giving reasons for denial of parole. Under pressure to do so, the board has begun to supply reasons. The purpose was that the inmate would know what further "treatment" he needed to be paroled next time. However, this reform has been abused, in that the reasons given are the general statutory ones (such as "release would be incompatible with the welfare of society") or the circular catch-all phrase: "additional institutional treatment is required to enhance the prisoner's capacity to lead a law-abiding life."[34] There has been much research questioning the existence of such "rehabilitative opportunities" in prison institutions. A multitude of studies have shown that prisons do not, and never did, contain much of a rehabilitative nature.[35] There are, then, important contradictions between theory and practice.

Criteria for Parole

Until very recently an inmate had to submit to "treatment" or he would not be paroled. To the extent he submitted and became "cured," he was supposed to get out. Did he? What are the signs that indicated to the board that he was cured? Was rehabilitation the real factor taken into account in the parole decision-making process? What other factors played a part, and how much of a part?

For example, it is interesting to note the relationship between rates of recidivism for particular crimes and rates of parole. It has been acknowledged that persons convicted of sex offenses have a very low rate of recidivism and thus would appear to be very quickly "cured," with a high rate of "success" on parole. However, because these crimes have been judged to have a high rate of "seriousness," such inmates are not released particularly early. This would indicate that not only rehabilitation, but punishment, is a factor. This punishment is cloaked in the language of protection of society, even though the risk of repetition of the particular crime is small. In 1923 S.B. Warner, a criminologist who studied the parole process, pointed out that there was little relationship between the board's criteria for release and the behavior of the men after release. This still holds true.[36]

It is the intent of this study to determine what criteria are actually used by the U.S. Board of Parole in making a parole decision. To do this, it is necessary to know what criteria the board says it uses in making a decision. This is not a simple task, since by law, as pointed out earlier, the criteria are very broad and general and the board has only recently begun to operationalize them. Many persons and groups have objected to the total discretion given the board, and have insisted on knowing the specific factors taken into account.[37] Previous researchers who wanted to investigate the process of parole had to try to decipher the board's criteria from case studies or rely on what the board suggested informally that it considered. There was no way of knowing the weight given to various factors. Researchers were also told that there was no such thing as board policy and that members function as individuals,[38] even in light of constant references in board statistics and quotations to "matters of policy."[39] This is another important contradiction.

Thus, to identify board criteria for parole, an investigation was undertaken of various lists and statements the board has published since 1971, along with the conclusions of researchers who have studied the process of parole since 1923, all of which indicate some of the important factors used in making parole decisions. These sources and criteria are indicated in Appendix 1A. Conspicuous by their absence, particularly in the new 1974 guidelines, are criteria relating specifically to treatment and rehabilitation. Perhaps the board has recognized the mythical nature of that element. We also noted that most of the criteria relate to the inmate's past. In fact, his "prognosis" for successful parole is based completely upon his past, as is the determination of time to be served. This is probably so because, indeed, most of the information available in an inmate's file is about his past, and prisons are there to punish people for that past.

The task was, then, to investigate to what extent the board actually used its established criteria. As an aid in gaining insight into this question, the case of an inmate who had recently appeared before the board and whose file we had access to was examined. It was hoped that reviewing this case would reveal some specific hypotheses that could then be tested by other means.

Appendix 1A:
Parole Decision Making

Criteria for Parole

Early studies of parole prediction, dating from Warner's study in 1923,[1] resulted in lists of attributes that discriminated between favorable and unfavorable parole outcomes. These would ostensibly also be the factors the board would want to consider in parole selection, as indicative of potential possibility of "risk" or recidivism:

The admission type

The history of probation or parole violations

Time free in the community without commitment

Prior records of commitment, sentences, and incarcerations

Prior juvenile-delinquency convictions

The employment history

The prison-custody classification

The punishment record and escape history

A prior history of mental hospital confinement

Aspects of the parole plan

Warner also listed various considerations that influenced the board in granting parole:

Whether a man had profited by his stay in the institution

Whether a man was so reformed that he was unlikely to commit another offense

Whether his conduct in the institution was good

Whether suitable employment was awaiting him on release

Whether he had a home or other proper place where he could go

His ability to tell the truth when questioned by the board

The seriousness of his offense and circumstances under which it was committed

His appearance when interviewed by the board

His behavior on former parole, if applicable

13

Warner related data he had gathered regarding success on parole to the criteria applied by the board, and suggested that there appeared to be little or no foundation for many of the board's assumptions. It appeared that the board did not act based upon information regarding success rates. There was little relationship between the board's criteria and the behavior of the men after release.

Paul Thomas, in 1962,[2] studied parole-selection and release procedures. He noted that these took place within both a formal system of rules, regulations, statutes, and norms, and an informal system of attitudes, sentiments, customs, and values. He included among the formal factors:

The nature of the inmate's offense

His criminal record

Physical and psychological reports

Attitude reports

Institutional conduct and time served

The proposed parole plan

The family's attitude

Community sentiments

A prediction table (perhaps)

But he pointed out that these formal considerations were interrelated with the board member's own values, experiences, and assumptions.

In its Biennial Report for July 1, 1968 to June 30, 1970, the factors the Board uses to make decisions are given as:

Sentence data

Facts and circumstances of the offense

Prior criminal record

Changes in motivation and behavior

Personal and social history

Institutional experience

General adjustment

Community resources, including release plans

Results of scientific data and tools

Comments by the hearing member or examiner

Length of sentence imposed by the courts

The board encourages the understanding that each case is considered on its individual merits: "Adults with definite sentences serve approximately the same period of time as those with indeterminate sentences. This probably reflects the fact that the Board considers each prisoner as an individual and paroles him at the most propitious time regardless of his official status" (p. 23).[3]

In its next Biennial Report for July 1, 1970 to June 30, 1972, the board deleted its specific delineation of criteria, and summed up in paragraph form some of the factors it takes into consideration:

The offense

The sentence

The prior criminal history

Behavior changes

Personal and social history

The institutional experiences

Community resources available

General personal adjustment

Scientific tools and data used in diagnosis and description of the prisoner

The scientific "selective factors" developed by the research study on decision making (which have made the parole decision even more refined)

The statement comparing determinate and indeterminate sentences is gone from the later report. However, it does include similar indications that individual concerns are important: "[The indeterminate sentence] makes it possible for the Board to make exceptions to the traditional one-third restriction (statutory parole eligibility is maximum sentence imposed), in cases where a prisoner is especially deserving or where unusual circumstances occur during the running of the term. In practice the Board makes a determination of optimum time for release without regard to the type of sentence imposed by the court, relying instead on the individual's needs and other relevant factors affecting the particular prisoner."

In a pamphlet entitled "You and the Parole Board,"[4] issued in January 1, 1971 for the edification of the inmate population, the important factors in deciding to parole are given as:

Type of offense

Length and seriousness of prior record

Family history

Marital situation

Emotional stability

Vocational and professional skills

Education

Age and physical condition

Living habits in the free community

Community resources

Behavior and progress during confinement (p. 4)

How the board plans to measure such variables as emotional stability, living habits, and progress during confinement is not discussed. Nor is it indicated what weights are given to the various indicators. The pamphlet also points out that "you are not exactly like any other inmate of this institution, [and] your hearing will not be just like anyone else's. The Board is interested in your needs as an individual human being. . . ." (p. 3)

From the information this pamphlet contains, it is possible to discern other general considerations the board takes into account. "Changes in the individual's family situation, his personal attitude, his age, newly acquired skills are also given appropriate weight. The amount of time which has elapsed between past offenses and the nature of the offenses are also studied. . . . The Board focuses its attention on the individual's parole plan in the community. . . . The man who has obtained more education and acquired a new job skill can present two good reasons for his release on parole. . . . The marital situation is a positive reason for parole if the marriage is healthy, a negative factor if it is stormy or unstable; divorce while he is incarcerated does not automatically argue for or against parole. . . . Your release plan should include a suitable residence, a verified offer of employment, and usually an approved parole advisor. . . . The Board is interested in your having *suitable* residence; there is no rigid rule which requires that you be paroled to your home if you have one, or that you cannot be paroled if you do not. . . . The U.S. Attorney who prosecuted your case and the Federal judge who sentenced you are invited to make recommendations regarding parole; these recommendations are submitted to the Board prior to your first hearing and are part of the material the Board considers. . . . Forfeited good time indicates that institution rules have not been observed and the Board's policy is to postpone its decision until such time as the statutory good time has been restored. . . . Persons judged to be psychotic are of course poor parole risks. . . . The recommendation by the institution staff is always given thoughtful consideration" (pp. 4-9). Throughout the pamphlet, the board encourages the inmates to believe that their case will be considered on an individual basis, that is, "The needs of the individual are the deciding factor. . . . Since no man's situation is just like another man's, factors of importance in one case won't even be considered in another" (pp. 3, 4).

In 1971, in response to pressure to operationalize the very broad and general statutory criteria for parole, the board issued a statement of Standards and Forms:[5]

General Factors in Parole Selection

A. Sentence data

  (1) Type of sentence
  (2) Length of sentence
  (3) Recommendations of judge, United States attorney, and other responsible officials

B. Facts and circumstances of the offense

  (1) Mitigating and aggravating factors
  (2) Activities following arrest and prior to confinement including adjustment on bond or probation, if any

C. Prior criminal record

  (1) Nature and pattern of offenses
  (2) Adjustment to previous probation, parole, and confinement
  (3) Detainers

D. Changes in motivation and behavior

  (1) Changes in attitude toward self and others
  (2) Reasons underlying changes
  (3) Personal goals and description of personal strengths or resources available to maintain motivation for law-abiding behavior

E. Personal and social history

  (1) Family and marital
  (2) Intelligence and education
  (3) Employment and military experience
  (4) Leisure time

(5) Religion
(6) Physical and emotional health

F. Institutional experience

    (1) Program goals and accomplishments in areas:
        (a) Academic
        (b) Vocational education, training, or work assignments
        (c) Recreation and leisure-time use
        (d) Religion
        (e) Therapy
    (2) General adjustment:
        (a) Interpersonal relationships with staff and inmates
        (b) Behavior, including misconduct
    (3) Physical and emotional health, and treatment

G. Community resources, including release plans

    (1) Residence; live alone, with family, or others
    (2) Employment, training, or academic education
    (3) Special needs and resources to meet them

H. Use of scientific data and tools

    (1) Psychological and psychiatric evaluations
    (2) Pertinent data from the uniform parole-reporting system
    (3) Other statistical data
    (4) Standardized tests

In a 1972 study done by the National Council on Crime and Delinquency (NCCD) in conjunction with its parole decision-making study, questionnaires were sent to state and federal parole board members, asking them to indicate factors they considered in granting parole. Examples of items considered very important were the adequacy of the parole plan, presence of a past record of assaultive offense, the offender's present family situation, the attitude of the inmate's family toward him, and the use of weapons in the offense. Considered as unimportant was any statistical prediction of the likelihood of parole violation.[6]

In an address before the National Conference on Criminal Justice, Washington, D.C., January 24, 1973, Maurice Sigler, chairman of the U.S. Board of Parole, stated that the recently conducted study of parole decision making by the NCCD resulted in the identification of three primary factors used in making parole-selection decisions. These were (1) the severity of the offense, (2) parole prognosis, and (3) institutional performance.[7]

These three factors have been incorporated into the board's 1974 guidelines for parole decision making, where they constitute a general policy regarding time to be served before release. The guidelines (see Table 1A-1) consist of a table, with six categories of "offense severity" and four categories of parole prognosis (risk). For each category of risk (also called "offender characteristics" and "salient [favorable] factor score"), there is indicated a range of time in months to be served before release. All of these time ranges are for those individuals who have made a "good" institutional adjustment. Factors considered important (salient) in predicting success on parole (as measured by remaining out of prison) are similar to those factors determined by earlier and current parole prediction studies to be of some significance (see Table 1A-2):[8]

No prior convictions

No prior incarcerations

Age at first commitment 18 years or older

Commitment offense did not involve auto theft

Never had parole revoked or been committed for a new offense while on parole

No history of heroin, cocaine, or barbiturate dependence

Has completed 12th grade or received GED

Verified employment or full-time school attendance for a total of at least six months during last two years in the community

Release plan to live with spouse and/or children

Note that none of these factors has anything to do with treatment and rehabilitation in or out of prison.

In another section (2.19) of its new Rules and Regulations, the board includes a list of factors, some of which "in the exercise of its discretion, the Board generally considers," along with "such others as it may deem appropriate." These are:

A. Sentence data

    (1) Type of sentence
    (2) Length of sentence
    (3) Recommendations of judge, United States attorney, and other responsible officials

B. Present offense

    (1) Facts and circumstances of the offense

    (2) Mitigating and aggravating factors

    (3) Activities following arrest and prior to confinement, including adjustment on bond or probation, if any

C. Prior criminal record

    (1) Nature and pattern of offenses

    (2) Adjustment to previous probation, parole, and confinement

    (3) Detainers

D. Changes in motivation and behavior

    (1) Changes in attitude toward self and others

    (2) Reasons underlying changes

    (3) Personal goals and description of personal strength or resources available to maintain motivation for law-abiding behavior

E. Personal and social history

    (1) Family and marital history

    (2) Intelligence and education

    (3) Employment and military experience

    (4) Physical and emotional health

F. Institutional experience

    (1) Program goals and accomplishments
        (a) Academic
        (b) Vocational education, training, or work assignments
        (c) Therapy

    (2) General adjustment
        (a) Interpersonal relationships with staff and inmates
        (b) Behavior, including misconduct

G. Community resources, including release plans

    (1) Residence; live alone, with family, or others

    (2) Employment, training, or academic education

    (3) Special needs and resources to meet them

H. Results of scientific data and tools

    (1) Psychological tests and evaluations

    (2) Statistical parole-experience tables (salient-factor score)

I. Paroling policy guidelines as set forth in section 2.20 (of these Rules and Regulations)

J. Comments by hearing examiners; evaluative comments supporting a decision, including impressions gained from the hearing

This appears to be the same as the 1971 list, with the deletion of F(c) Recreation and leisure-time use, F(d) Religion, and F(3) Physical and emotional health, and treatment. The paragraph on the use of scientific data and tools has been reworded to include their new guidelines. They have also added comments by hearing examiners and impressions gained from the hearing.

In sum, it is apparent that the board has never really indicated the process by which decisions to parole or deny are made. In none of their lists and publications are we given any indication of what items are weighted more heavily or considered to be more important and central to their task. There are obviously a greater number of factors given than could be seriously considered in a five to ten minute cursory review of an inmate's file before a hearing. We are not even certain of a relationship between criteria and remaining out of prison. And what has happened to rehabilitation? Such lists serve to mystify rather than clarify. It would appear that the board is not interested in clarification but, rather, in maintaining its discretionary power. The recent issuance of guidelines in response to criticism suggests that a predetermined time to be served according to the alleged seriousness of one's crime is of prime importance, and that other criteria serve as "fillers" or rhetoric, designed to satisfy inquiring social scientists and other concerned persons.

Notice of Action

The following form illustrates the U.S. Board of Parole Notice of Action regarding the case of Olivia Sanchez and the various factors considered relevant to decision making. She was not paroled, even though the report states a decision outside the guidelines appears warranted.

Table 1A-1

U.S. Board of Parole Rules and Regulations

ADULT
Guidelines for Decision Making
Average Total Time Served before Release
(Including Jail Time)

Form R-3
(Rev. 1/75)

Offense Characteristics: Severity of Offense Behavior (Examples)	OFFENDER CHARACTERISTICS: Parole Prognosis (Salient Factor Score)			
	Very Good (11-9)	Good (8-6)	Fair (5-4)	Poor (3-0)

Low
Immigration-law violations
Minor theft (includes larceny and simple
  possession of stolen property less than
  $1,000)
Walkaway
	6-10
	months
		8-12
		months
			10-14
			months
				12-16
				months

Low-Moderate
Alcohol-law violations
Counterfelt currency (passing-possession less
  than $1,000)
Drugs:
  Marijuana, simple possession (less than
    $500)
Firearms act, possession-purchase-sale (single
  weapon-not altered or machine gun)
Forgery-fraud (less than $1,000)
Income-tax evasion (less than $10,000)
Selective Service Act violations
Theft from mail (less than $1,000)
	8-12
	months
		12-16
		months
			16-20
			months
				20-25
				months

Moderate
Bribery of public officials
Counterfeit currency (passing-possession
  $1,000-$19,999)
Drugs:
  "Hard drugs," possession by drug user (less
    than $500)
  Marijuana, possession with intent to distrib-
    ute-sale (less than $5,000)
  "Soft drugs," possession with intent to dis-
    tribute-sale (less than $500)
Embezzlement (less than $20,000)
Explosives, possession-transportation
Firearms Act, possession-purchase-sale (altered
  weapon(s), machine gun(s), or multiple
  weapons)
Income-tax evasion ($10,000-$50,000)
Interstate transportation of stolen-forged
  securities (less than $20,000)
Mailing threatening communications
Misprision of felony
Receiving stolen property with intent to resell
  (less than $20,000)
Smuggler of aliens
Theft-forgery-fraud ($1,000-$19,999)
Theft of motor vehicle (not multiple theft or
  for resale)
	12-16
	months
		16-20
		months
			20-24
			months
				24-30
				months

Offense Characteristics: Severity of Offense Behavior (Examples)	OFFENDER CHARACTERISTICS: Parole Prognosis (Salient Factor Score)			
	Very Good (11-9)	Good (8-6)	Fair (5-4)	Poor (3-0)

High
  Burglary or larceny (other than embezzlement)
    from bank or post office
  Counterfeit currency (passing-possession
    $20,000 or more)
  Counterfeiting (manufacturing)
  Drugs:
    "Hard drugs" (possession with intent to dis-
      tribute-sale by drug user to support own
      habit only)
    Marijuana, possession with intent to dis-
      tribute-sale ($5,000 or more)
    "Soft drugs," possession with intent to dis-
      tribute-sale ($500-$5,000)
  Embezzlement ($20,000-$100,000)
  Interstate transportation of stolen-forged secu-
    rities ($20,000-$100,000)
  Mann Act (no force—commercial purposes)
  Organized vehicle theft
  Receiving stolen property ($20,000-$100,000)
  Theft-forgery-fraud ($20,000-$100,000)

High row values: 16-20 months | 20-26 months | 26-32 months | 32-38 months

Very High
  Robbery (weapon or threat)
  Drugs:
    "Hard drugs," possession with intent to dis-
      tribute-sale for profit (no prior conviction
      for sale of "hard drugs")
    "Soft drugs," possession with intent to dis-
      tribute-sale (over $5,000)
  Extortion
  Mann Act (force)
  Sexual act (force)

Very High row values: 26-36 months | 36-45 months | 45-55 months | 55-65 months

Greatest
  Aggrevated felony (e.g., robbery, sexual act,
    aggrevated assault)—weapon fired or per-
    sonal injury
  Aircraft hijacking
  Drugs:
    "Hard drugs" (possession with intent to dis-
      tribute-sale) for profit (prior conviction(s)
      for sale of "hard drugs")
  Espionage
  Explosives (detonation)
  Kidnapping
  Willful homicide

Greatest characteristics note: (Greater than above—however, specific ranges are not given due to the limited number of cases and the extreme variations in severity possible within the category)

Notes: 1. These guidelines are predicated upon good institutional conduct and program performance.
      2. If an offense behavior is not listed above, the proper category may be obtained by comparing the severity of the offense behavior with those of similar offense behaviors listed.

Table 1A-1 (cont.)

3. If an offense behavior can be classified under more than one category, the most serious applicable category is to be used.
4. If an offense behavior involved multiple separate offenses, the severity level may be increased.
5. If a continuance is to be given, allow 30 days (1 month) for release-program provision.
6. "Hard drugs" include heroin, cocaine, morphine or opiate derivatives, and synthetic opiate substitutes.

Table 1A-2

Notice of Action—Part II—Salient Factors

R-2 part 2
(Rev. 4/74)

Case Name _____ Register Number _____

Item A
  No prior convictions (adult or juvenile) = 2   _____
  One or two prior convictions = 1
  Three or more prior convictions = 0

Item B
  No prior incarcerations (adult or juvenile) = 2   _____
  One or two prior incarcerations = 1
  Three or more prior incarcerations = 0

Item C
  Age at first commitment (adult or juvenile) 18 years or older = 1   _____
  Otherwise = 0

Item D
  Commitment offense did not involve auto theft = 1   _____
  Otherwise = 0

Item E
  Never had parole revoked or been committed for a new offense while on   _____
      parole = 1
  Otherwise = 0

Item F
  No history of heroin, cocaine, or barbiturate dependence = 1   _____
  Otherwise = 0

Item G
  Has completed 12th grade or received GED = 1   _____
  Otherwise = 0

Item H
  Verified employment (or full-time school attendance) for a total of at least 6 _____
      months during the last 2 years in the community = 1
  Otherwise = 0

Item I
  Release plan to live with spouse and/or children = 1   _____
  Otherwise = 0

Total Score   _____

Offense Severity: Rate the severity of the present offense by placing a check in the appropriate category. If there is a disagreement, each examiner will initial the category he chooses.

Low _____   High _____

Low Moderate _____   Very High _____

Moderate _____   Greatest _____

                                               (e.g. willful homicide, kidnapping)

Jail Time (Months) ___ + Prison Time (Months) ___ - Total Time Served To Date ___ Months

Guidelines Used: _____ Youth _____ Adult _____ NAHA

Tentative Decision _____

Parole Form H-7
(Rev. May, 1976)

UNITED STATES DEPARTMENT OF JUSTICE
United States Parole Commission
Washington, D. C. 20537

Notice of Action

Name _____ Olivia Sanchez _____

Register Number _____ *Institution* Calif.
Institution for Women

In the case of the above-named the following action with regard to parole, parole status, or mandatory release was ordered:

CONTINUE FOR AN INSTITUTIONAL REVIEW HEARING IN JUNE, 1975.

(Reasons for continuance or revocation) (Conditions or remarks)

Your offense behavior has been rated as very high severity. You have a salient factor score of 10. Guidelines established by the Board which consider the above factors indicate a range of 26-36 months to be served before release for Adult cases with good institutional program performance and adjustment. You have been in custody a total of five (5) months. After careful consideration of all relevant factors and information presented, it is found that a decision outside the guidelines at this consideration appears warranted because: First offender, no evidence of narcotic usage, stable employment record, no further difficulty while on bond, stable home, excellent institutional adjustment. You need additional institutional treatment, specifically, academic, vocational and counseling

Appeals procedure: You have a right to appeal a decision as shown below. Filing the appeal is your responsibility which others cannot perform for you. Forms for that purpose may be obtained from your caseworker, or the Regional Office of the Commission, and must be filed with the Commission within thirty days of the date this Notice was sent.

A. Decision of a Hearing Examiner Panel. Appeal may be made to the Regional Commissioner.
B. Decision of the National Commissioners when referred to them for reconsideration. Appeal may be made to the Regional Commissioner.
C. Decision of the Regional Commissioner. Appeal may be made to the National Appeals Board.
D. Decision of National Commissioners in cases where they assumed original jurisdiction. Appeal may be made to the entire Commission.
E. Decision of a Regional Commissioner relative to Parole condition or continuance under supervision. Appeal may be made to the National Appeals Board.

Copies of this notice are sent to your institution and/or your probation officer. In certain cases copies may also be sent to the sentencing court. You are responsible for advising any others to whom you might wish to make information on this form available.

August 9, 1974 _____ Western _____
(Date Notice sent)   (Region) (NAB) (Nat. Dir)   (Docket Clerk)

INMATE COPY

FPI LC 6-76 846C SETS 9471

2

The United States of America vs. David Donner

The Case

On June 13, 1968 David Donner, a 27-year-old male, and two other men, all wearing red wigs, went to the residence of Alice Smith[1] on Coronado Island near San Diego. Two of the men went in and one waited outside. Mrs. Smith was held with a 22-caliber pellet gun pointed at her head, and photographed in this position with a Polaroid camera. She was beaten and her life threatened, and one of the men gave her an injection of an unknown drug, which left her unconscious. She later awakened, bound by the wrists with tape. The men then drove to the Bank of America, Coronado Branch. Two men went in and one waited outside. They went over to the desk of Vice-President and Manager Jack Smith, and showed him the photograph of his wife with a gun pointed at her head. Smith was advised that a holdup was in progress and that his wife was being held hostage and would be killed if everyone in the bank did not cooperate fully. The men took $50,000 from the bank vault and left. They were observed leaving in a 1954 beige Buick. Approximately one-half hour later, two special agents observed their car, gave chase, and apprehended the one man inside. They found three red wigs, a 22-caliber pistol, a Polaroid camera, and $50,000 in cash.

The case of the *United States of America* vs. *David Donner* is examined in great detail below. We follow the processing of Donner's case through the courts, prisons, and finally to the parole board, on which we focus.

The assumptions and mode of operation of the U.S. Board of Parole are relatively unknown and secret. Therefore, looking at an actual case dealt with by the board should illuminate our understanding of what goes on. Case studies serve primarily as a stimulus for eliciting hypotheses and providing insight into social processes and practices in instances where there is little research experience or information to go on.[2] The case of David Donner raises some basic issues and illustrates some specific features of the parole structure and process, which is examined by other methods in subsequent chapters. Documents regarding the case are listed in Appendix 2A.

The Court

In 1969 David Donner and two other men were tried in federal court for the crime of bank robbery. They were convicted. One of the men cooperated with

27

the government and gave information about the other two. He received a 4-year sentence. The other two, including Donner, received a 15-year sentence.

At the time of trial, Donner presented a defense of insanity. He said he had participated in the robbery because he believed that if he did not do it he would be killed by the mafia "mob" that was after him. Psychiatric tests conducted before the trial indicated that he did have severe psychiatric problems, and he was diagnosed as "schizophrenic with paranoid reactions." However, his defense of insanity was rejected and he was convicted and sent to McNeil Island Federal Penitentiary in Washington.

Because he was indigent at the time, the court appointed an attorney to represent him in his appeal of the decision. In 1971 Donner's conviction was reversed because of a change that had occurred in the rules regarding instructions to the jury, and the case was returned to the district court for retrial. A new trial was set for January 1972. Donner was released on bail, pending the second trial. He returned to Milwaukee, Wisconsin, where he was from originally.

By this time Donner had been in prison for two years. Although his attorney felt he had a very valid psychiatric defense, he did not want to risk a second trial and possible recommitment for 15 years. Therefore, a plea-bargaining agreement was entered into, wherein Donner agreed to plead to a lesser charge, bank larceny, and go back to prison for a 90-day psychiatric study. If the study showed that he no longer experienced the psychiatric problems he had in 1968 and 1969, the judge would seriously consider granting him probation. The government was willing to enter into this plea bargain for what was considered a most heinous crime because while Donner was in prison, he had accomplished some "miraculous" things, according to the prison authorities. The warden at McNeil Island had written to the judge saying that Donner was "the most rehabilitated prisoner we have ever had in the history of this penitentiary." Donner had started an X-ray Radiology Department at McNeil, and had gotten his national license as an X-ray technician, the first person who had ever done so. The warden also pointed out in his letter that during a strike, Donner had come to the aid of the administration. Letters supporting Donner's probation came from McNeil Island's chief medical officer, his caseworker at McNeil, and the radiologist who had in 36 years written supporting letters for only four persons.

While out on bond, pending his second trial, Donner had gotten a job as an X-ray technician in a hospital in Milwaukee. He became so well respected by the staff, and was considered such a valuable and capable employee, that several persons wrote letters of recommendation for him to the judge. Such persons included the chief radiologic technologist, the chief radiologist, and a general physican affiliated with the hospital. The letters indicated that if Donner were given probation, he would become chief X-ray technician of the hospital. While free on bail, Donner also attended some group-therapy sessions at a community-counseling center, where he had impressed the group supervisors to a great extent with his interactional abilities. They, too, wrote letters to the judge, supporting the granting of probation. Donner was seen by a psychiatrist at the Neuropsychiatric Institute, UCLA, who pronounced him tremendously improved with no psychosis.

In 1972 Donner returned to California and pled guilty, according to the plea-bargain agreement. He was sent to Terminal Island Federal Correctional Institution, San Pedro, for a 90-day psychiatric study. While there for only a short time, he so impressed the medical staff that they, too, wrote supporting letters to the court. Such letters came from the assistant hospital administrator, the senior medical officer, and the senior staff surgeon. The psychiatrist who did the 90-day study reported that, indeed, Donner had probably been psychotic in 1968, but that he had made a complete recovery and should be placed on probation and not incarcerated again. Donner also received a positive report from his caseworker. It was pointed out that this was his first arrest and conviction, and that his emotional problems were probably due to serious family difficulties in his personal life.

After the 90-day psychiatric study, Donner returned to court for sentencing. The Bureau of Prisons had written the judge, upon being informed of the impending sentence of probation. The letter talked about "clinical findings" in their own staff evaluation of Donner. These findings indicated that Donner was still an "anxious, emotionally unstable individual with sociopathic tendencies and with limited insight into his past behavior. He continues to use his long-standing defense mechanisms of denial and projection and attempts to present himself in the most favorable light." This latter observation is most interesting, since this is obviously what someone being "rehabilitated" in prison would do to demonstrate positive results of the program. The Bureau of Prisons recommended that "because of the gravity of this offense, we are recommending that Mr. [Donner] be sentenced to a term of ten years under the flexible provisions of 180 USC 4206 (a) (2) which would provide for immediate Parole Board review and an extensive period of supervision in the community after release." Donner would be encouraged to continue his "obvious progress in preparing himself for eventual release."

The judge sentenced Donner to ten years.

Motion for Reduction of Sentence

Donner was returned to prison. One hundred twenty days later, his attorney filed a motion for reduction of sentence with the district court. The motion was heard before another judge, since the original judge was on vacation. The second judge, based upon the same facts and information presented earlier before the first judge, decided to grant the motion for reduction, and put Donner on probation. He was thereupon released.

About 45 days later, the government prosecutor realized that the motion for reduction of sentence, although mailed on the 120th day, had actually been received on the 122nd day, two days too late according to the law for any action to have been taken legitimately. Therefore, the prosecutor made a motion to reimpose the ten-year sentence and send Donner back to prison. The judge, reluctantly, was forced to rescind his order of probation and the earlier sentence was reimposed. Donner's attorney filed an appeal of this order with the court of appeals, and Donner remained free on bond pending this hearing.

The higher court realized that the law was firm as far as filing dates were concerned, and knew that the sentence of probation was invalid. However, the court recognized the fact that the district court wanted Donner placed on probation, and based on the facts, agreed with it. Therefore, to circumvent the issue of late filing, the appellate court asked the prosecutor to write the U.S. Board of Parole and request that they have a parole hearing to parole Donner, thus ending the matter. At first, the parole board refused to hear the case because Donner was not in custody and that would be contrary to procedure since they had never heard a case where an individual was not in custody. It was arranged that Donner would go into custody in the federal marshall's office in Milwaukee (where he was living) at 9:00 a.m. on the day of the parole board hearing, and would be released at 5:00 p.m., still on bail, regardless of the outcome of the hearing. Thereupon, a hearing was held in Washington, D.C. between Mr. Sherman, the attorney for Donner, and three members of the parole board.

The Parole Board

From the transcript of that hearing, we are able to follow the parole board in operation, note its basic assumptions, and observe the method by which parole decisions are made. Specifically, we look for what criteria are considered important in making a determination, and, in fact, which factors are considered at all.

The first four and one-half pages of the transcript below indicate the board's concern with setting precedents and judicial interference. The discussion centers around their reluctance to hear any case where the individual is not in custody. We are including a somewhat extensive portion of the transcript of the hearing because it is rare that such hearings are held, and because the operations of the parole board are unknown and secret, and therefore access to their documents is also rare.

U.S. Board of Parole Washington Review Hearing for David Donner, November 6, 1973

The case of David Donner comes before a panel of the board composed of George J. Reed, Gerald E. Murch, and Thomas E. Holsclaw at 10:00 a.m.,

November 6, 1973, at the board's Hearing Room, Washington, D.C., John Sicoli, board analyst, recording the hearing. Donner is represented by Victor Sherman of Los Angeles, California, as attorney of record.

Mr. Reed: You are the attorney of record of David Donner. The records show he is serving a ten-year 4208(a) (2) indeterminate sentence for bank larceny. He had originally been sentenced to 15 years under conspiracy to commit bank robbery and a study was done by the Federal Bureau of Prisons and a report was made back to the court resulting in a ten-year sentence being imposed by Judge Turrentine. The record shows there was considerable litigation in this matter, bringing it to us, I might say Mr. Sherman, in a most unusual and precedent-setting manner. In the 20 years I have been associated with this board, we have not heard a man for parole who was not in custody and we are doing that in this case at the request of the 9th circuit court of appeals, where this order was entered on July 24, 1973, by the three judges of the 9th circuit court of appeals. So the record might be complete, I think it would be well to have the record indicate that the court records show that "[Donner] did commit a heinous crime." I am quoting now from the circuit court's decision, "but the District Court believes him thoroughly rehabilitated and does not want him incarcerated. The statute precludes the court from reconsideration now because of the lapse of time. Naturally, the Board is a little shy, fearing a precedent. It does seem to us that when a court requests in such unusual circumstances that a parole be considered in advance of incarceration, the Board will not be setting a dangerous precedent if it is so done only on a request of a court. We respect the Board's right to pass its own independent judgment on the circumstances, but we doubt its position of insisting or possibly ruining the balance of a man's whole life because of its technicalities. Thus, we make the order we do. It should be noted that altogether [Donner] has been incarcerated about twenty-five months. The United States Attorney is requested to attempt to secure a Parole Board Hearing for [Donner] on his application for parole without the incarcerating requirement. The government somehow should be flexible enough to accommodate itself to the needs of this case." I'm quoting a part of the 9th circuit court of appeals, July 24, 1973, decision. I think one other comment I would like to make in opening is that the original sentence was given by Judge Turrentine and the change of sentence by Judge Nielsen occurred at a time when apparently Judge Turrentine was out of the country, if I understand the record correctly. Is that correct?

Mr. Sherman: Yes, that's correct.

Mr. Reed: Well, I think that sets the record on the case, and at your request, and I would say at the request of the 9th circuit court of appeals, this board is entering into a new precedent in this hearing and I think the records should so show.

Mr. Murch: Mr. Reed, I don't think this precedent should go beyond this case as far as this board is concerned. You made it very clear there that we were hearing it at the insistence of the 9th circuit court.

Mr. Reed: That's right.

Mr. Murch: So we are glad to do that, but as I look down the road, whether it be an income-tax violator or any bank robber or anything else, they could never have to serve a day in prison before the board had to pass on cases under the indeterminate provision. And, I don't think this is fair at all. I don't think the public expects that and certainly I will not be a party to it.

Mr. Reed: I accept Mr. Murch's comments and stand to correct the record that the very act of complying with the order of the 9th circuit is in itself a precedent. I don't think it becomes a precedent for this board, one that this board would follow without further appeal in the future. I think that's what Mr. Murch is saying. With that introduction and having now established the record, we are willing and, at your request and the request of the 9th circuit court, happy to hear from you, Mr. Sherman.

Mr. Sherman: Thank you. Just for the record, in fact, Mr. Donner is in custody so this board is not hearing a case where the man is not in custody.

Mr. Reed: That was my next question. Where is he now in custody?

Mr. Sherman: He went into custody this morning in Milwaukee, Wisconsin.

Mr. Reed: Is he in custody with the United States marshal?

Mr. Sherman: That is correct.

Mr. Reed: When did he go into custody there?

Mr. Sherman: He went into custody at 8 o'clock this morning.

Mr. Reed: That would be Midwest time.

Mr. Sherman: That's correct. So he's been in custody for I guess about an hour.

Mr. Reed: The letter requires that he remain there until 5 o'clock tonight.

Mr. Sherman: That's correct. The U.S. attorney in San Diego, to be sure we did not set any precedent before this board and did not violate this board's internal regulation, asked if I would agree to have him go into custody so he would be in custody at the time the board heard this matter, and I agreed, and so he has gone into custody.

Mr. Reed: The board is aware of that, and that was my next question to you, and I'm glad you have covered that so the fact that we are hearing a man in custody of the United States marshal does not make the precedent it would have otherwise.

Mr. Sherman: That's correct.

Mr. Reed: Very well.

Mr. Sherman: Even though, as you are aware, the 9th circuit did not ask that that be done, I thought, to come within the regulations of the board, that would be appropriate.

Mr. Reed: All the 9th circuit did was to request the United States attorney to negotiate with this board.

Mr. Sherman: That's correct.

We note the reference made for the record on page 1 of the transcript, that "[Donner] did commit a heinous crime." We also note the statement that "the District Court does not want him incarcerated." These indicate some assumptions and considerations the board has recognized.

The hearing proceeded to a discussion of Donner's exceptional prison performance, which was supported by letters from the warden and other administrative officers at McNeil Island Federal Penitentiary. This was followed by a discussion of Donner's accomplishments since being released on bail one year previously, supported by letters from the doctors in Milwaukee, from co-workers at two hospitals where Donner worked, and from Milwaukee newspaper clippings about Donner's contributions to the community. Donner's attorney reviewed the history of the case, and pointed out that the Bureau of Prisons had recommended the maximum sentence originally, "due to the severity of the crime," and not because of any individual considerations. This would now appear to be "unfair." The board, in return, pointed out certain negative interpretations that could be made based upon the psychiatric report of the 90-day study and the Bureau of Prison's "clinical" evaluations.[3] Donner's attorney pointed out that based upon Donner's accomplishments in prison and his demonstrated "rehabilitation," the judge of the district court had reduced his sentence to probation and felt that being in prison could serve no further purpose. The board was only hearing the case because of a technicality, because the motion for modification was filed two days late and parole would be the easiest way out for the courts. The district court judge had written to the parole board himself, explaining the case, and notifying them that he felt very strongly about releasing Donner.

At this point it is helpful to summarize the arguments used in favor of paroling Donner.

Psychiatric Evaluations Made in 1968 and 1972
Indicating Recovery from Mental Illness

The diagnosis made in 1968 and 1969 was that of "schizophrenic reaction, paranoid type, presently in remission." Directly after the robbery, Donner spent approximately five months in various hospitals, during which time he was said by the doctors to have recovered from his previous illness. In 1972 the psychiatric studies indicated that Donner was "paranoid schizophrenic in remission, with sociopathic personality improved." The recommendation of the final psychiatric report was that "Mr. [Donner] not be kept in prison but once outside he should actively be involved in psychiatric treatment of an insight oriented nature and should be steadily employed."

Performance in Prison

Donner was a "model" prisoner. His letters of recommendation support his claim to be "the most rehabilitated prisoner ever seen at McNeil Island." To be able to set up a radiology department and acquire a national license as an X-ray technician while in prison is no small accomplishment, especially if one had no such training before entering prison. The prison staff agreed.

Performance in the Community while Out on Bail

Donner began working in a hospital in Milwaukee as soon as he was released in September 1972. At the time of the parole hearing (November 1973), he had two jobs in two different hospitals, one as chief X-ray technician, in which capacity he worked from 7:00 a.m. to 3:30 p.m., and another in the radiology department of a second hospital, where he worked from 4:00 p.m. to 11:30 p.m., in charge of the night shift. Administrators, doctors, nurses, and technicians of both hospitals had composed and signed letters supporting Donner's work, encouraging the board to parole him. Donner's salary in one year had increased from $4,800 a year to $17,000 a year. Donner had also remarried and had a stepchild by this marriage. Several articles appeared in the Milwaukee newspapers regarding Donner's work for the community, primarily in a hospital that served a minority group. One of the articles also included a photograph of Donner. His mother had just been honored as the most outstanding citizen in the community. A senator in the Wisconsin legislature wrote to the parole board on behalf of Donner stating that he would be personally responsible for him upon release.

Letter from the District Court Judge

The judge wrote: "I must state to you that in neither my experience as a state court judge or as a United States district judge have I ever seen such a complete rehabilitation on the part of a defendant. I therefore unhesitatingly and unqualifiedly recommend that you place him on parole at this time, without the service of any additional time of incarceration . . . if you grant him parole and he doesn't live up to it, I will publicly acknowledge any blame in that regard."

Support from Court of Appeals

The three-judge panel of the court of appeals, by requesting the parole board to hear this case in a most unprecedented manner, knowing that their action might be interpreted as interfering with the board's independent status, which was guarded quite carefully, in effect supported the district court judge and Donner. In its order to the board, the appellate court said:

We respect the Board's right to pass its own independent judgment on the circumstances, but we doubt its position of insisting on possibly ruining the balance of a man's whole life because of its technicalities. . . . The United States attorney is requested to attempt to secure a Parole Board hearing for [Donner] on his application for parole without the incarceration requirement. The government somehow should be flexible enough to accommodate itself to the needs of this case.

Donner Had Received an "a" Number

Donner had been sentenced under the (a)(2) provision by the first judge, meaning that his was an indeterminate sentence with no minimum and that he was eligible for parole at any time.

Results of the Parole Board Hearing

Donner's attorney returned from Washington on the same day of the parole hearing. He found a telegram from the parole board awaiting him (see Figure

2-1). Parole was denied. In making their decision, the factors that appeared to be significant were:

1. The fact that a codefendant was still in custody and paroling Donner would not be "fair"
2. The fact that Donner had not served the 55 to 65 months customarily served according to their new guidelines by an individual who had committed his "type" of offense and who had his "score" on parole prognosis
3. The belief that it was necessary for further punishment to occur because of the severity of the crime
4. Reluctance to set a precedent in granting paroles based upon hearings suggested by the judicial branch of government

The following pages from the transcript indicate that these were the prime considerations. Are they, however, the same factors the board has formally and informally acknowledged as criteria in its selection process?

Mr. Sherman: And, I will close with this, what would be the purpose for putting him back in. It certainly can't be to rehabilitate him. There couldn't be any reason to do that. I don't see any and I'm sure the board doesn't wish to be punitive.

"RUWLRBQ/VICTOR SHERMAN ATTY AT LAW 8383 WILSHIRE
BLVD SUITE 510 BEVERLY HILLS CALIF 90211
RUWLRBQ/WARDEN FEDERAL CORRECTIONAL INSTITUTION
TERMINAL ISLAND CALIF
DJJUSD
BT
UNCLAS
RE: DONNER, DAVID

ON NOVEMBER 6, 1973, THE U.S. BOARD OF PAROLE HAS ISSUED THE
FOLLOWING ORDER IN THE CASE OF DAVID DONNER, (THE BOARD
FINDS THAT AS OF NOVEMBER 6, 1973, MR. DONNER IS IN THE CUS-
TODY OF THE U.S. MARSHAL, MILWAUKEE, WISCONSIN UNTIL 5:00
P.M. NOVEMBER 6, 1973 AWAITING DISPOSITION OF THIS HEARING). THE
BOARD HAS HEARD MR. DONNER'S COUNSEL AS REQUESTED BY THE 9TH
CIRCUIT COURT OF APPEALS AND HAS CONCLUDED THAT IN THE INTER-
EST OF EQUITY, JUSTICE AND FAIRNESS AS RELATED TO THE CODEFEND-
ANTS OF BOARD ORDERS THAT THE CASE BE CONTINUED FOR AN INSTI-
TUTIONAL REVIEW HEARING SIX MONTHS AFTER RETURN TO CUSTODY.
PLEASE ADVISE MR. DONNER OF BOARD ACTION. BY COPY ALL INTER-
ESTED PARTIES ADVISED THIS ACTION.

Figure 2-1. Notice of Board Action-1

Mr. Murch: Why not? Wasn't a woman's life threatened? Didn't she have a gun at her head? This is all a matter of didn't they commit a bank robbery and put lives in jeopardy? Now, this is a very serious matter. We're talking about fairness . . . what about Rogers who's sitting up there in McNeil Island, while this man has been out on the street. Is that fairness?

Mr. Sherman: There were three people involved, one of whom has been released other than Mr. Donner. There were three people involved.

Mr. Reed: A shorter sentence, however.

Mr. Sherman: Yes, he was given a four-year sentence.

Mr. Murch: That was different.

Mr. Sherman: The only reason he was given a four-year sentence was because he agreed to testify against the other two. Now, if we want to call that fair or not. . . . They just plucked one of the three and said okay now you testify; it wasn't because he was less culpable.

Mr. Murch: We could argue that.

Mr. Sherman: All right, but I am a defense attorney, and I often have defendants cooperate and they are given a lesser sentence, so I am not unhappy with that situation. But, as far as punitive, he was in jail a total of 25 months already. I looked through your statistics by the way, and for a crime of this nature, if you have an excellent work record within the institution, the average length of stay is supposedly, although I was shocked to hear this, 30 months.

Mr. Reed: Where did you get that statistic?

Mr. Sherman: I have the tables, your new guidelines, though I always understood it to be much longer. This is from your Pilot Regionalization Project average total time served before release, and it's from category E, very high severity offenses, armed robbery, criminal act, weapons, social act, etc.

Mr. Reed: That was a preliminary draft that was at the very next session reviewed as were many other offenses. And, it moved up into the highest offense category where there was armed force or where there was any kind of force used. What I'm saying is, subsequent to the initial accountability factor which you're quoting from a research project, that offense carries and has carried through much of the project and now is a policy of the board to carry, a 55 to 65 months' sentence.

Mr. Sherman: You have 55 to 65 months here, but I thought it was rated depending upon your prognosis, your institutional performance, and your high probability of parole outcome.

Mr. Reed: Right, that is true.

Mr. Sherman: So the highest is 55 to 65 months if your parole outcome is favorable.

Mr. Reed: You missed my point—in another group below, there is a new category of offenses of the greatest severity that has been added since that original.

Mr. Sherman: There's another category that's not on here?

Mr. Reed: Yes, that's right and that's what I'm trying to say to you, and that group is life termers; those are murderers, those are skyjackers, and so forth. There now is a new group, and in that group is any armed bank robbery or any robbery where there is aggressive or assaultive behavior—where there is a discharge of a gun or where there is assaultive behavior involved in the act; and surely this one will fall into that category. The wife was assaulted at the time and was at her home when the picture was taken, and if you're using our guidelines and I've done a workup on our guidelines in this case, it would have to fall beyond 65 months to be within our guidelines.

Mr. Sherman: I see.

Mr. Reed: I had very particularly worked up the guidelines from the research project. The original report did not have the definitive breakdown that it has acquired over the last year and a half.

Mr. Sherman: I see. Well, the only thing I can say is, do we want to just punish Mr. Donner, because in 1968 when, whether he was legally insane or not, he certainly had very severe psychiatric problems, everybody agrees on that; he did the one criminal act in his life. . . . Since then everybody who has seen him seems to agree that he's recovered and we have seen his performance. . . . If we want to say that if you did something in 1968 and we know that you were sick, now five years later you have shown us what you can do and you served, actually he's served more than 25 months, but let's say a little over two years in prison, and if we're going to say okay that counts for nothing, the only thing is you haven't served the 55 months or 65 months that our guidelines say, therefore, you have to go back and do it, what's the incentive for anybody to try and rehabilitate themselves in prison?

Mr. Reed: I don't think that we said just that, but I think we said there are guidelines. One of the things that Mr. Murch has eluded to is the codefendant Rogers. I took time to review the comparability of Rogers and Donner as to social background and there is even more going for Rogers as far as no prior record and he certainly is not as culpable. And, in all of the standards that we would want to gauge it by, I would say he came before a different judge, Judge Smith, and he, as you stated, did not have as qualified an attorney as Donner did at the first trial or as competent an attorney as counsel now representing him today. As you stated earlier, through plea bargaining there was a reduction in sentence and this board does have a problem, if I may suggest it to you, in trying to determine when one judge sees this case as being all good, and another judge seeing his codefendant as a case requiring some accountability in the public's interest, we have a real question here the board's got to wrestle with in this case and I recognize everything that you said in terms of the progress this man's made in the time he has been out. But, we do have under the third statutory criteria that you're referring to, 4203 of Title 18, a problem on the question of practicing disparity. Now plea bargaining has a bad way of doing this and when handling the cases of Rogers or the case of White or your client, you get into a tremendous amount of differential treatment here in the handling of these three cases, despite all of the factors that you have very ably covered here this morning. So ours is not an easy position that we are in this morning, and on the other hand Judge Nielsen has very strong feelings and has a right to express those within the time he has jurisdiction but after that jurisdiction expires, then to insist that these cases be treated differently. . . . Judge Nielsen could have looked at these other cases in which . . . I think he had some obligation to observe the records of these other cases . . . the question of equity and justice would have been better served in my humble judgment. I understand there are technical and legal problems as to how you would do this but it leaves us with a very, very difficult question in equity.

Mr. Sherman: Well, I understand that and all I can say is, I suppose every judge might handle hundreds of criminal cases. They look at codefendants, what did they do, and try to make some comparative judgment. I would urge that we use the 4-year sentence just as much as the 15-year one because the only reason they got that of course is cooperation. I might add this: the original judge that sentenced these people, Judge Williams, had been on the bench about three months when he originally sentenced these people. If this case came up today, who knows what his sentence might be if we presented all these factors.

Mr. Reed: But, Rogers has done equally well at McNeil Island as Donner. He has made an outstanding record and, amazingly, in almost the same field.

Mr. Sherman: Is that correct?

Mr. Reed: Yes, that parallelism is amazing. Well, that is the problem the board is faced with here in this sort of a situation and you have properly stated and very ably stated the merits of your client.

Mr. Sherman: Can I say this: don't you think if we sent Mr. Donner back that it would be a discouraging element to other inmates. Suppose, Mr. Donner went back at this time and he talked to his fellow inmates and he told them his whole history—this must be a fairly unique case, . . .

Mr. Murch: But, he has brought all this on himself with your cooperation and the court's cooperation. He had this sentence and if he served this sentence he would have had it. Now, I just can't buy the idea that it's a tremendous experience because he asked for it, up to this point.

Mr. Sherman: I'm sorry, what do you mean, asked for it?

Mr. Murch: I say to go back before the court to have his case reviewed, and the psychiatric study, and release on bail, and all of the rest of it; if he had been like Mr. Rogers and served his sentence, that would have been it; it would have been no experience along that line.

Mr. Sherman: Oh, I understand that but the fact is all these things have happened and he has shown what he can do, and whether or not he had a legal right to ask for all of these benefits, he has been able to take advantage of them. And, what I'm saying is, if he went back into an institution now and would talk to his fellow inmates and tell them his story and say that I've been out for 14 or 15 months and I have done all these great things and I did these things at the institution, well . . .

Mr. Murch: Mr. Rogers, what would he say? I sat and "rot," the word you used, for 45 months.

Mr. Sherman: I would think that, well, Mr. Rogers may or may not have a legitimate complaint and perhaps he also ought to be paroled.

Mr. Murch: I think what I'm saying is, I think a parole board should be fair and equitable in handling cases.

Mr. Sherman: Of course.

Mr. Murch: I think this is one of our primary functions.

Mr. Sherman: But, isn't one of the . . .

Mr. Murch: When you get into a situation where one man serves a shorter time and another one a long time for the same type of offense, no prior record can say that I'm rehabilitated too.

Mr. Sherman: But the point I'm making is, if we are to encourage rehabilitation, isn't it anti-rehabilitation even though we want to be fair to Mr. Rogers, to say to Mr. Donner, even though you have obviously demonstrated rehabilitation it's more important that you serve some comparable sentence with your codefendant.

Mr. Reed: But I say that this is our real, tough problem that the board has to wrestle with. I guess, if I were Mr. Rogers, I would say that I should have had the court appoint Mr. Sherman as my attorney, and I should have appeared before Judge Nielsen. There are serious circumstances that come into play here. Could I just take a moment to read a short summary of the parole examiner who heard Rogers' case on October 17, 1973, at McNeil Island: "Subject was committed to the institution initially and has made an outstanding institutional adjustment. He has maintained a clear conduct record, has been involved in some college level courses. Above all, in terms of institutional adjustment, he has been the principal individual in the institution's hospital laboratory. He now holds the title Hospital Chief Serologist. Work reports and list of accomplishments during the course of his work performance cover a full page of highest commendations. He has passed several examinations in Number Organization relating to his laboratory proficiency and expertise. The institution advises that subject's performance saves approximately one hundred thousand dollars per year in laboratory services and the institution computes its savings to the government of approximately sixty-six thousand dollars per year for his work performance. His work and performance are of such quality that the Bureau of Prisons is interested in retaining him, and employment has been offered at a GS-7 level at the Terminal Island Institution." I just want you to get a little bit of the understanding of what this board is up against in trying to understand how to be fair with Rogers and with your client, as well as the other matters. But, here is a man, and it's amazing how they parallel in their professional interests and accomplishments.

Mr. Sherman: Maybe they encouraged each other when they were at McNeil together.

Mr. Reed: Could be.

Mr. Sherman: I might add that Mr. Donner was also offered employment at McNeil Island in the same way.

Mr. Reed: I think the parallelism in the two cases is amazing.

Conclusion

What can we learn from the case of David Donner? We have here a sample of parole board decision making. The arguments and choices made here are representative of the selection process. Using the board's own guidelines for decision making,[4] we can compute Donner's score (as Mr. Reed pointed out the board also did). The total points possible for the parole prognosis or salient-factor score (offender characteristics) is 11. There are nine salient factors (see Table 2-1).

The second consideration in the guidelines is institutional performance. The given time ranges to be served are for those inmates whose institutional adaptation is good. Donner's performance was unique and exceptional.

The third consideration is the crime for which the individual was incarcerated. In Donner's case this was bank *larceny*, which would fall in the severity category, "very high severity offenses."[5] The range of time to be served for an individual with a salient-factor score of 9 to 11 points is 26 to 36 months. Donner had already served 25 months. However, the board was dealing with Donner in terms of his crime as reported in the files rather than with the crime to which he pled and for which he was incarcerated. As evidenced in the transcript, the board placed him in the "greatest severity" category and determined that for that offense he must serve 55 to 65 months (even though on their guidelines no range for this category is given, but merely the statement that information is not available due to the limited number of cases). No consideration was given to the fact that Donner had been sentenced under section 4208 (a)(2), which was an indeterminate sentence without a one-third minimum, given by a judge for the very purpose of allowing parole at any time "rehabilitation" should occur.[6]

Table 2-1
Salient Factor Score

	Donner's Score
1. No prior convictions	2
2. No prior incarcerations	2
3. Age at first commitment	1
4. Commitment offense did not involve auto theft	1
5. Never had parole revoked or had been committed for a new offense while on parole	1
6. No history of heroin, cocaine, or barbiturate dependence	1
7. Has completed 12th grade or has received GED	1
8. Verified employment (or full-time school attendance) for a total of at least 6 months during last 2 years in the community	1
9. Release plan to live with spouse and children	1
	11

Epilogue

The Court of Appeals

Donner's attorney requested an *en banc* hearing before all eight members of the parole board, which was agreed to and scheduled for a date three months ahead.

Meanwhile, Donner's attorney informed the appellate court that the board had denied parole. The chief judge of the court of appeals telephoned the district court judge who had reduced the sentence. The appellate court had made the decision to remand the case back to him and allow Donner to withdraw his original plea of guilty, on the grounds that to refuse to do so would be a miscarriage of justice.[7] The district court judge then conferred with the government prosecuting attorney, who finally decided just to withdraw his objection that the filing was two days late and agree that the motion for reduction of sentence was indeed timely filed. The sentence of probation then held, and Donner was not reincarcerated.

The parole board held a hearing three months later and affirmed their previous decision to deny parole. (See Figure 2-2.)

```
                                                          TELETYPE
          MAR 1, 1974     Nasatir, Sherman & Hirsch
 162 528 (17017 MSCWL 736121)
 RATUZYUW RUEBWJA2561 2571500-UUUU—RUWLREG.
 ZNB UUUU
 R 2614572 FBB 74
 FM STEVE B. JOHNSTON, PAROLE EXECUTIVE DEPT OF JUSTICE WASH DC
 TO RUWLREQ (VICTOR SHERMAN) ATTORNEY AT LAW, NASATIR, SHERMAN*
 HIRSCH, 8383 WILSHIRE BLVD, SUITE 510, BEVERLY HILLS, CALIFORNIA
 90211 TELE: (213) 653-3303
 ZEN/INFOR TO ASSISTANT U. S. ATTORNEY JAMES W. MEYERS, SAN
 DIEGO, CALIFORNIA.
 ZEN/INFO TO WARDEN, FEDERAL CORRECTIONAL INSTITUTION, TERMINAL
 ISLAND CALIFORNIA.
 DJJIDC
 BT
 UNCLAS
 RE: DONNER, DAVID

 ON FEBRUARY 25, 1974, THE BOARD VOTED TO CONTINUE THE CASE OF
 DAVID DONNER, WITH AN INSTITUTIONAL REVIEW HEARING ON THE
 NEXT DOCKET AFTER HIS RETURN TO FEDERAL INSTITUTION. PLEASE
 NOTIFY MR. DONNER, BY COPY, ALL PARTIES NOTIFIED THIS ACTION.
 GWP
 ET
 *2561
```

Figure 2-2. Notice of Board Action-2

Since 1973 Donner has worked in the two hospitals in Milwaukee, developing their radiology facilities. He has not had any problems with the law.

The case of the *United States* vs. *David Donner* raises many important questions regarding the selection process of the U.S. Board of Parole. The major issue concerns the criteria the board actually used in making its decision to deny parole. It is questionable whether they applied their own established, or even statutory, criteria. Donner's perfect score on parole prognosis would indicate that his release was not incompatible with the welfare of society, and that there was a reasonable probability that he would live and remain at liberty without violating the laws. Donner did more than just observe the rules of the institution in which he was confined. Donner's positive psychological reports, supportive letters from co-workers and employers, and his achievements as an X-ray technician all indicate "rehabilitation." What it comes down to is a question of "offense severity" and its corresponding "amount of time to be served."

The reasons why the board refused to parole Donner do not appear in their established guidelines, particularly the pivotal issue of the codefendant still serving time. In fact, the board encourages the belief that each case is considered on its own individual merits. Factors that do appear in the guidelines and lists of criteria were not even considered.

Although we can discern certain important characteristics about the operation of an institution from a detailed case study, there are limits[8] to the generalizations and predictions that can be made based upon it. Therefore, to investigate further the apparent contradiction between established criteria and operational criteria used in decision making, an extended study was undertaken. The next chapter contains an analysis of 7,286 cases of inmates who appeared before the board for a parole hearing, with the intent of finding out to what extent the board uses its own criteria and/or what criteria it actually uses.

Appendix 2A:
The Case of David Donner:
Documents

The following documents are available in the case files:

A. Psychiatric Evaluations:

Letter from Medical Director, Brentwood Hospital, Veterans Administration, Los Angeles, 1968
Diagnosis of Brentwood Hospital, 1968
Evaluation of John Robuck, M.D., 1969
Hospital Discharge Summary, University Hospital of San Diego County, 1968
Diagnosis of Drs. Langyel and Hepner, 1968
Bureau of Prisons Classification Study, 1972
Evaluations of Drs. Kane and Schmitz, Counseling Center, Milwaukee, Wisconsin, 1971, 1972
Evaluation of John Suarez, M.D., UCLA Neuropsychiatric Institute, 1972
Bureau of Prisons Letter to Judge Turrentine, 1972
Bureau of Prisons Classification Study and Staff Evaluation, 1972

B. Letters from the Community:

Dr. James Kelley, Northwest General Hospital, Milwaukee, Wisconsin, 1972
Paul Dadian, Chief Radiologic Technologist, Northwest General Hospital, 1972
Dr. Thomas Roskos, Northwest General Hospital, 1972, 1973
Staff Members, Northwest General Hospital, 1973
Personnel Director, Misericordia Community Hospital, Milwaukee, Wisconsin, 1973
Payroll Department, Northwest General Hospital, 1973
James Devitt, Senator, Wisconsin Legislature, 1972
Newspaper Article, Milwaukee, Wisconsin, 1973

C. The Prisons

Letter of Recommendation, Henry Kyle, M.D., Chief Medical Officer, McNeil Island Federal Penitentiary, 1972
Letter of Recommendation, David Hirt, M.D., McNeil Island, 1971
Letter of Recommendation, Bruce Miller, M.D., McNeil Island, 1971
Letter of Recommendation, Spanish Instructor, McNeil Island, 1971
Letter of Recommendation, Michael Kaslow, M.D., McNeil Island, 1972

45

Letter of Recommendation, Mr. Macy, McNeil Island, 1972

Letter of Recommendation, Michael Bettmann, M.D., McNeil Island, 1972

Letter of Recommendation, E.M. Lucero, Assistant Hospital Administrator, McNeil Island, 1972

Letter of Recommendation, C.B. LaRoe, Case Manager, McNeil Island, 1972

D. The Court

Judge Leland Nielsen, San Diego District Court to U.S. Board of Parole, 1972

Appellate Court Opinion, *United States of America* vs. *David Donner*, 1973

Eugene Barkin, General Counsel, U.S. Bureau of Prisons, to United States Attorney, Southern District of California, 1972.

3

A Quantitative Analysis of Decision Making

An inmate at the California Institute for Women at Corona told a group of visitors about her experience with the parole board. When she appeared before a panel of two board members, they told her that in order to be paroled she should go and seek Jesus. When she returned the next year for another parole hearing, she told the two members of that panel, who were different from the first, that she had found Jesus and that he was with her today. They told her to return when she felt she could make it independently, on her own.

An Analysis of Decision Making

The following analysis was undertaken to investigate the extent to which criteria established by the U.S. Board of Parole are actually relied upon by its members in making parole decisions. From the preceding case study, we see that the decision to deny parole was primarily based on (1) the issue of equity and fairness to the codefendant, and (2) the fact that Donner had committed a crime they considered very serious and therefore had to serve time proportionate to that severity. Sources examined earlier (see Appendix 1A) do not indicate that "codefendant still in prison" is a factor considered in making a determination. They do reveal that adjudged seriousness of the offense is a consideration, but we are not told that it is weighted so heavily as to exclude all other factors, particularly "rehabilitation." It would appear that the board's primary concern is to equalize punishment,[1] just the opposite of its statements in "You and the Parole Board,"[2] where it is indicated that "you are not exactly like any other inmate of this institution and your hearing will not be just like anyone else's," and "since no man's situation is just like another man's, factors of importance in one case won't even be considered in another."

The problem to be investigated, then, is whether factors claimed by the board to be those they consider in determining whether to parole or deny actually have some statistical power in explaining that decision. It is hypothesized that there is some degree of discrepancy between established criteria and their use. We investigate what the extent of that discrepancy is. We also attempt to determine what some of the criteria are that really matter.

The sample consisted of 7,286 inmates who appeared for a parole hearing before the U.S. Board of Parole in the period from November 1970 to June 1972. The data were gathered by the National Council on Crime and Delinquency (NCCD) Research Center at Davis, California, in collaboration with the U.S. Board of Parole and under a grant from the National Institute of Law Enforcement and Criminal Justice of the Law Enforcement Assistance Administration.[3] The population from which the sample was chosen included all cases considered for parole during that period. The data consisted of information regarding the background characteristics and past and present performance of these potential parolees.[4]

The NCCD sample consisted of 8,669 inmates. It was decided to exclude women and juveniles since there were not enough of these groups in the sample upon which to base any reliable analysis.[5] Also excluded were any cases that had missing data on the analysis variables or cases exhibiting uncorrectable coding errors. This brought the sample down to 7,286 cases.

Extracted from the data were indicators that matched the criteria established by the board. As the best representation of the board's criteria, their most recent guidelines, issued June 5, 1974[6] were used. The guidelines consist of three main elements: (1) a scale of severity of offense; (2) a score on a list of nine "salient factors," which supposedly indicate *parole prognosis* (risk to society or potential for "success" on parole); and (3) a range of time to be served. (See Table 1A-2 for list of the nine salient factors.) It is understood that the time ranges indicated in the guidelines are for those whose institutional performance has been "good." These guidelines are considered to be a more "scientific" way of proceeding than "individual case decision making," also known as the "clinical" approach, although the parole board members point out that both are needed in the decision-making process.[7] Each inmate who appears for a parole hearing is assessed in terms of these three factors. Using these guidelines, board members can point to what they see as "objective" scores on an instrument based on data collected "scientifically," thus justifying and legitimizing their decisions. "Offense severity" is generated by ranking offenses into six categories from "low" to "greatest" according to prevailing conventional wisdom regarding the seriousness of crimes.[8] "Salient-factor score" is created by summing an individual's points on nine items relating to his past background. This score supposedly indicates his *parole prognosis*, the element of risk to the general welfare of society if he were to be released, and his potential for remaining out of prison. Once a score is arrived at, the inmate is placed in a particular cell on the guidelines graph, depending on his offense and his prognosis score. The place on the graph where offense severity intersects with salient-factor score determines the time to be served.[9] In this way the board members have provided for the element of "fairness" in their decisions. However, in being "fair" and equalizing the very disparate sentences given by judges for the same crimes, the board has done away with the idea of individualized treatment and rehabilitation. Since they went to all the trouble of establishing specific periods to be served, it is unlikely that many decisions will be made outside the guidelines.[10]

An investigation of the guidelines was undertaken to determine whether the three elements of offense severity, time to be served, and salient-factor score, were the factors that explained the decision outcome to parole or deny for the 7,286 inmates in the NCCD sample. If a large amount of the variance was explained by these factors, this would indicate that the guidelines were based on the past experience of the board and that the board had been operating according to the criteria and ranges of time indicated there.

Table 3-1 indicates the way in which the three elements that constitute the guidelines have been organized by the board. Each inmate in the sample was placed in one of the categories of offense severity, according to the crime for which he was convicted.[11] Inmates were also scored on the nine salient factors, which were then summed, and each person was placed in the appropriate cell of the resulting cross-classification displayed in Table 3-1.

It was then asked whether the inmates in our sample had been released on parole after having served time in prison relative to their "offense severity" and "salient-factor score." To do this, each cell of the guidelines was subdivided into three parts relative to "time served": (1) whether the inmate had served time *less than* that indicated on the guidelines, (2) whether he had served time *within* that indicated on the guidelines, or (3) whether he had served time *greater than* that indicated on the guidelines. Table 3-2 indicates the number and percentage of inmates, paroled and not paroled, falling within each of the cells on the classification matrix, and whether they served time "less than," "within," or "greater than" the time range indicated.

As Table 3-2 indicates, large percentages of inmates who served *less* time than the range specified on the guidelines were up for parole. Most were not

Table 3-1
Guidelines for Decision Making: Average Time Served before Release

	Offender Characteristics Salient Factor Score[a] (Probability of Favorable Parole Outcome)			
Offense Characteristics	9-11 Very High	6-8 High	4-5 Fair	0-3 Low
Low severity	6-10[b]	8-12	10-14	12-16
Low-moderate severity	8-12	12-16	16-20	20-25
Moderate severity	12-16	16-20	20-24	24-30
High severity	16-20	20-26	26-32	32-38
Very high severity	26-36	36-45	45-55	55-65
Greatest severity	—[c]	—	—	—

[a]For an understanding of how salient factor score is computed, see table 1A-2.
[b]Entries represent number of months.
[c]Information not available due to limited number of cases.

Table 3-2

Percentages of Inmates Paroled or Not Paroled Serving Time Less than, Within, or Greater than the Guidelines Indicate

Offense Characteristics		(9-11) L	W	G	(6-8) L	W	G	(4-5) L	W	G	(0-3) L	W	G
Low severity	P %	28.6	0	42.9	7.5	0	8.7	3.9	2.0	2.0	25.0	0	0
	N	(2)		(3)	(6)		(7)	(2)	(1)	(1)	(1)		
	NP %	28.6	0	0	78.7	4.9	0	76.5	5.9	9.8	7.50	0	0
	N	(2)			(63)	(4)		(39)	(3)	(5)	(3)		
Low to moderate severity	P %	5.3	10.7	38.0	17.3	8.3	13.7	7.9	4.1	9.1	2.4	2.4	7.3
	N	(8)	(16)	(57)	(90)	(43)	(71)	(27)	(14)	(31)	(1)	(1)	(3)
	NP %	34.0	7.4	4.7	49.7	3.7	7.3	56.0	7.6	15.2	70.2	9.7	7.3
	N	(51)	(11)	(7)	(258)	(18)	(38)	(191)	(26)	(52)	(29)	(4)	(3)
Moderate severity	P %	34.4	8.6	9.3	16.4	7.9	11.0	12.5	2.2	8.8	8.0	0.8	4.0
	N	(52)	(13)	(14)	(110)	(53)	(74)	(78)	(14)	(55)	(20)	(2)	(10)
	NP %	41.7	2.0	4.0	52.6	5.3	6.7	58.5	4.6	13.3	66.9	6.0	14.4
	N	(63)	(3)	(6)	(352)	(36)	(45)	(366)	(29)	(83)	(168)	(15)	(36)
High severity	P %	27.5	5.0	8.1	20.3	4.2	10.9	13.1	2.9	9.0	10.7	1.9	6.4
	N	(61)	(11)	(18)	(236)	(49)	(127)	(156)	(34)	(107)	(52)	(9)	(31)
	NP %	53.1	2.3	4.1	51.9	3.3	9.4	54.9	4.4	15.7	63.5	4.0	13.6
	N	(118)	(5)	(9)	(605)	(39)	(109)	(654)	(53)	(187)	(308)	(19)	(66)

Very high severity	P	%	18.3	4.8	7.1	12.9	3.2	11.2	6.8	2.2	9.6	9.2	1.0	7.1
		N	(23)	(6)	(9)	(84)	(21)	(73)	(31)	(10)	(44)	(9)	(1)	(7)
	NP	%	60.3	5.6	4.0	54.2	6.7	11.8	57.2	4.2	20.1	64.3	8.1	10.2
		N	(76)	(7)	(5)	(353)	(44)	(77)	(261)	(19)	(92)	(63)	(8)	(10)

Note: 1. The category "Greatest Severity" was combined with "Very High Severity" because of the small number of cases.

2. L = Time served less than the guidelines.
   W = Time served within the guidelines.
   G = Time served greater than the guidelines.
   P = Paroled.
   NP = Not paroled.
   % = Percentage of cell.
   N = Number in cell.

paroled. However, in many of the cells, *more* inmates were paroled who had served *less* time than those who had served times *within* or *greater than* indicated. The number and percentages of persons falling *within* the guidelines are very small. Of those inmates *within* the guidelines, in most cases more were not paroled than were paroled. Because of this, it would be difficult to conclude that the ranges of time indicated on the guidelines were based on the past practice and policy of the board. The pattern has not been to release on parole those inmates who have served time within the guidelines. In fact, if the ranges of time indicated on the guidelines are followed in the future, many of those who would have been released earlier may serve longer sentences, especially those inmates in the middle-severity ranges.

If we sum up the number of individuals paroled who served time *within* the ranges on the guidelines (298), we see that this figure is smaller than the number of persons paroled who served *more* time than indicated on the guidelines (742). In fact, the greater number of persons paroled served *less* time than indicated on the guidelines (1,049).

Of those individuals not paroled, a large number (4,023; 77%) had served *less* than the time indicated on the guidelines and would not be expected to receive parole. However, of all those *within* the guidelines, 344 or 54 percent of them were not paroled. Of those who had served *more* time than indicated, 830 or 53 percent were not paroled. Therefore, 1,174 (53%) persons who could or should have been paroled according to the guidelines were not paroled.

It appears, therefore, that the times to be served indicated on the guidelines are arbitrarily set, and that they are set higher than practice would indicate. An inmate may now know the time he can expect to serve, but in general, individuals will serve more time than they have in the past.

If the ranges of time to be served indicated on the guidelines did not come from actual past practice by the board, how were they arrived at? Why do they appear to be higher than practice would indicate? These are questions that must be answered by the board.

Let us return to the question asked earlier, with which we are primarily concerned, which is whether the factors included on the guidelines account for the outcome of parole decisions. As the previous discussion demonstrates, the ranges of time to be served specified on the guidelines are not related to parole decisions; that is, previous parole decisions do not appear to be based upon these amounts of time served in prison. To determine the predictive power of the elements of the guidelines as a whole, a statistical Lambda was computed for the 60 cells created and shown in Table 3-2. Lambda measures the association between two qualitative variables. It measures the reduction of error in prediction on the dependent variable from knowledge of the independent variable.[12] In this case, the dependent variable was parole decision: to parole, deny, or continue to a fixed date for further review (*limbo*). The independent variable was the 60 cells of the cross-classification matrix.

Lambda in this case was 0.133. The modal category of the sample was "continued to fixed date for rehearing," which is that category of the parole decision into which 45.8 percent of the cases fell.[13] By chance, we could classify inmates into this modal category and be correct 45.8 percent of the time. Thus, a Lambda of 0.133 indicates that we improve over chance by making 13.3 percent fewer errors, to the point of being able to predict correctly 59.1 percent of the dependent variable. This obviously leaves quite a bit of the decision-making process unexplained.

The predictive power of knowing the offense severity, the score on the nine salient factors, and the time served is not great. It would appear that other criteria are operating in the parole decision-making process.

Since an analysis of the predictive power of the board's guidelines left much of the variance regarding parole decision unexplained, a search continued for other predictors that might be operating in the process. Other factors mentioned by the board as having some effect on their decision were considered,[14] and indicators were obtained for 27 of them.[15] These are listed in Table 3-3. The first column indicates what the predictor is; the second column designates the possible categories of the predictor variable into which a case may fall; the third column specifies the percentage of the sample that fell into that category.

The technique used in the analysis of these variables was multivariate nominal analysis (MNA).[16] MNA is a series of parallel, multiple-classification analyses[17] performed on a nominal dependent variable with more than two categories; that is, the dependent variable is transformed into a set of binary variables (0-1 dummy variables) that are regressed on the predictors.

Multivariate nominal analysis generates several statistics: (1) the generalized squared multiple correlation (R^2), which indicates the percentage of the variance on the dependent variable explained by the independent predictor variables; (2) the multivariate theta (θ), which indicates the percentage of cases that could be correctly classified after taking into account each individual's score on the independent variables;[18] (3) the generalized eta squared (m^2); and (4) the bivariate theta (θ), which provide ways of measuring the strength of bivariate relationships, and which are analogous to (1) and (2) respectively; (5) the coefficients, which indicate the effects of membership in the particular category of the independent variable on the likelihood of membership in each category of the dependent variable; and (6) the adjusted percentages, which show in the case of each independent variable, for each category of the dependent variable, what the overall relationship is after holding the other independent variables constant.[19]

In this case the dependent variable was "parole decision," the possible categories of which were (1) parole (28.67%), (2) continued to expiration of sentence (25.50%), or (3) continued to a fixed date for rehearing (45.83%). The modal category was "continued to a fixed date." This means that by chance we

Table 3-3

Indicators of 27 Key Factors in the Board's Decision-Making Process

Variable Name	Code	Percentage of the Sample
1. Sentence type	1) Regular adult (court establishes release date—eligible for parole after serving 1/3 of sentence)	37.84%
	2) Indeterminate (parole at any time—"A-2" number)	31.55
	3) YCA (Youth Corrections Act)	22.39
	4) Other	8.22
2. Codefendant	0) No	47.38
	1) Yes	52.62
3. Parole revocations	0) No	74.61
	1) Yes	25.39
4. Total convictions	1) No prior convictions	0.03
	2) 1 or 2 prior convictions	24.79
	3) 3 or more prior convictions	75.19
5. Total incarcerations	1) No prior incarcerations	33.85
	2) 1 or 2 prior incarcerations	31.43
	3) 3 or more prior incarcerations	34.72
6. Juvenile delinquent	1) No	90.90
	2) Yes	9.10
7. Race	0) Nonwhite	29.19
	1) White	70.81
8. Marital status	1) Single	41.15
	2) Married	29.10
	3) Divorced	13.52
	4) Separated	11.84
	5) Common law	4.39
9. Grade claims	1) Less than high school	66.73
	2) High school diploma	25.38
	3) Higher education	7.89
10. Employment	1) Verified employment for six months in last two years of civilian life, or student or unemployable 75% of that time	51.30
	2) Employed less than six months in last two years of civilian life, and not student or unemployable 75% of that time	13.70
	3) Employment not ascertained	35.00
11. Family criminal record	0) No	73.52
	1) Yes	26.48
12. Mental hospital	0) No	91.55
	1) Yes	8.45
13. Homosexuality	0) No	96.09
	1) Yes	3.91

Variable Name	Code	Percentage of the Sample
14. Military discharge	0) No military history	61.39
	1) Honorable discharge	21.97
	2) Other than honorable discharge	13.15
	3) Other	3.49
15. Alcohol	0) No use	42.55
	1) Use	57.45
16. Drug use	0) No use	63.63
	1) Marijuana	21.56
	2) Heroin, cocaine, or barbiturates	11.60
	3) Other	3.21
17. Custody classification	1) Maximum	31.97
	2) Medium	32.13
	3) Minimum	35.90
18. Custody level reduced	0) No	74.84
	1) Yes	25.16
19. Job training	0) None or unknown	71.60
	1) Less than or equal to five months	11.36
	2) More than five months	17.03
20. Education program	0) No or unknown	57.04
	1) Yes	42.96
21. Prison punishment	0) No	77.35
	1) Yes	22.65
22. Planned living arrangement	1) With parents or guardian	32.45
	2) With wife and/or children	24.40
	3) With paramour	4.50
	4) With others	16.84
	5) Alone	8.07
	6) No plans	13.74
23. Offense severity	1) Low severity	1.95
	2) Low to moderate severity	14.42
	3) Moderate severity	23.29
	4) High severity	42.04
	5) Very high severity	16.90
	6) Greatest severity	1.40
24. Car thief	0) No	74.76
	1) Yes	25.24
25. Age	2) 18 to 26	42.11
	3) 27 to 35	30.33
	4) 36 and over	27.56
26. Length of sentence	1) Up to 12 months	7.01
	2) 13 to 24 months	13.72
	3) 25 to 36 months	15.41
	4) 37 to 48 months	6.90
	5) 49 to 60 months	13.33
	6) 61 to 120 months	34.07
	7) 121 to 180 months	5.11
	8) 181 months and over	4.45

Table 3-3 (cont.)

Variable Name	Code	Percentage of the Sample
27. Time served out of total sentence	1) 0 to 10%	17.95
	2) 11 to 30%	33.54
	3) 31 to 50%	32.65
	4) 51 to 60%	7.14
	5) 61% and over	8.72
Dependent Variable:		
Parole decision	1) Parole	28.67
	2) Continued to expiration	25.50
	3) Continued to fixed date	45.83

could correctly classify individuals into the category "continued to fixed date" (the modal category) and be correct 45.83 percent of the time. If the criteria the board has identified actually matter in their decision making, they should explain a larger portion of that decision.

After regressing parole decision on the 27 predictor variables listed in Table 3-3, MNA's generalized R^2 was 0.3825, indicating that 38 percent of the variance is explained by the 27 predictors. About two-thirds of the variance still remains unexplained. From this, it can be inferred that the board members are making up their minds based on other considerations.

The multivariate theta statistic was 0.7122, indicating that 71 percent of the cases can be correctly classified from the 27 predictors. However, since by chance we could predict accurately about 46 percent of the time, and since approximately 46 percent of the sample fell in the category "continued to fixed date," we have only improved our predictive ability by about 25 percent over chance. If the board adhered to its established criteria, we would have expected to be able to improve our prediction level much closer to 100 percent. There are still other undisclosed factors operating in the decision-making process.

Turning to the bivariate statistics, the analysis revealed, through the generalized etas squared and bivariate thetas, only a mild association between any independent variable and the parole decision. This is indicated in Table 3-4.

The strongest association occurs for the variables time served out of total sentence, length of sentence, and custody classification. There is some association for the variables sentence type, custody level reduced, job training, and offense severity. For the other 20 variables, the association is extremely weak, indicating little relationship between them and the parole decision. There is little or no improvement over chance knowing values on these variables. Knowing nothing whatsoever, one could predict decision outcome accurately in about 46 percent of the cases, so the most one has improved is 11 percent knowing the

Table 3-4
Generalized Eta Squared and Bivariate Theta Scores for the 27 Predictors and Parole Decision

Predictor	Generalized Eta Squared	Bivariate Thetas
Sentence type	0.0749	0.5224
Codefendant	.0034	.4583
Parole revocations	.0000	.4583
Total convictions	.0055	.4583
Total incarcerations	.0184	.4583
Juvenile delinquent	.0006	.4583
Race	.0021	.4583
Marital status	.0076	.4583
Grade claimed	.0028	.4583
Employment	.0050	.4583
Family criminal record	.0001	.4583
Mental hospital	.0008	.4583
Homosexuality	.0007	.4583
Military	.0020	.4583
Alcohol	.0006	.4583
Drug use	.0104	.4583
Custody classification	.0960	.5556
Custody level reduced	.0520	.5215
Job training	.0415	.5018
Education	.0164	.4583
Prison punishment	.0005	.4583
Living arrangement	.0338	.4583
Offense severity	.0273	.4704
Car thief	.0012	.4583
Age	.0213	.4583
Length of sentence	.1361	.5699
Time served out of total sentence	0.1597	0.5283

length of sentence received. Even in this case, there is still 43 percent of the outcome unexplained.

We can now look at the effects of membership in a particular category of an independent variable on the likelihood of being paroled or not. These effects are indicated by the coefficients listed in Table 3A-1.[20]

Larger coefficients appear in various cells of the following predictor variables: sentence type, total convictions, total incarcerations, custody classification, custody level reduced, job training, prison punishment, living arrangement, offense severity, age, sentence, and time served out of total sentence.

Coefficients for the other variables are small and do not extend beyond 3.80 in any cell and differences between cells are not great. Therefore, they have little or no effect on decision outcome.

Sentence type has an effect primarily on the categories continued to expiration and continued to fixed date. For example, those who are sentenced under the Youth Corrections Act are 5 percent less likely than others to be continued to a fixed date, 3 percent more likely to be continued to expiration, and 3 percent more likely to be paroled than the average inmate.

Those who have no convictions are 25 percent less likely to be paroled and 23 percent more likely to be continued to a fixed date. However, this coefficient is based on only two cases, since only two persons of the sample had no prior convictions, and should therefore be interpreted as very inconclusive. Those with no prior incarcerations are 6 percent more likely to be paroled and 6 percent less likely to be continued to expiration. Those with three or more previous incarcerations are 7 percent less likely to be paroled and 8 percent more likely to be continued to expiration. Those classified under maximum security have a 12 percent less likelihood of being paroled, a 6 percent greater likelihood of being continued to expiration and 5 percent greater likelihood of being continued to a fixed date. Those classified under medium security have a 5 percent less likelihood of being paroled; those classified under minimum security have a 15 percent greater likelihood of being paroled, an 8 percent less likelihood of being continued to expiration, and 8 percent likelihood of being continued to a fixed date. Those whose custody level has been reduced have a 5 percent greater likelihood of being paroled. Those who are involved in job training for more than five months while in prison have a 13 percent greater likelihood of being paroled; those who have had less than five months have a 5 percent less likelihood of being paroled; and those who have had no training at all in prison have a 2 percent less likelihood of being paroled. Those with more than five months job training also have a 4 percent less chance of being continued to expiration, and a 9 percent less chance of being continued to a fixed date. Those with a record of prison punishment have an 8 percent less likelihood of being paroled, a 4 percent greater likelihood of being continued to expiration, and a 4 percent greater likelihood of being continued to a fixed date.

Regarding living arrangement, those who plan to live with their parents after release have a 3 percent greater chance of being paroled. Those who plan to live with spouse and/or children have 0.17 percent *less* likelihood of being paroled, a 3 percent less likelihood of being continued to expiration, and a 3 percent greater likelihood of being continued to a fixed date. Those who plan to live with a paramour have a 4 percent less likelihood of being paroled; those who have no plans for living arrangement upon release have an 11 percent less likelihood of being paroled, a 5 percent greater likelihood of being continued to expiration, and a 6 percent greater likelihood of being continued to a fixed date. Regarding offense severity, those whose crime falls in the category "low severity" have a 5 percent greater likelihood of being continued to expiration and a 5 percent less likelihood of being continued to a fixed date. (This is probably due, as the board has said, to the fact that those who commit what are considered less serious crimes get lighter sentences and serve them out.) Those whose crime falls in the range of "very high severity" have a 6 percent less chance of being paroled, and a 5 percent greater chance of being continued to expiration. Those whose crime is in the greatest severity category have a 4 percent greater likelihood of being continued to expiration. Those whose age is in the range from 18 to 26 have a 2.47 percent greater likelihood of being paroled and are 6 percent less likely to be continued to expiration. Those who are over 36 have a 6 percent greater likelihood of being continued to expiration and a 3 percent less likelihood of being paroled.

Thus far, the coefficient percentages and any differences between them across categories and cells are quite small. For two variables, however, sentence and time served out of total sentence, the coefficients are greater. Those who receive a sentence of up to 12 months have a 24 percent less likelihood of being paroled, a 61 percent greater likelihood of being continued to expiration, and a 37 percent less likelihood of being continued to a fixed date. Those with a sentence of from 13 to 24 months have an 11 percent less likelihood of being paroled, a 37 percent greater likelihood of being continued to expiration, and a 25 percent less likelihood of being continued to fixed date. Those with a sentence of from 25 to 36 months have a 5 percent less likelihood of being paroled and a 6 percent greater likelihood of being continued to expiration. Those with a sentence of from 37 to 48 months have a 3 percent less likelihood of being paroled, a 2 percent less likelihood of being continued to expiration, and a 6 percent greater likelihood of being continued to a fixed date. Those with a sentence of from 49 to 60 months have an 8 percent less likelihood of being continued to expiration, and a 6 percent greater likelihood of being continued to a fixed date. Those whose sentences range from 61 to 120 months have an 8 percent greater likelihood of being paroled, a 17 percent less likelihood of being continued to expiration, and a 9 percent greater likelihood of being continued to a fixed date. Those with sentences of from 121 to 180 months have an 11 percent greater likelihood of being paroled, a 29 percent less likelihood of being continued to expiration, and an 18 percent greater likelihood of being continued to a fixed date. Those with sentences of over 180 months have a 15 percent greater likelihood of being paroled, a 34 percent less likelihood of being continued to expiration, and a 19 percent greater likelihood of being continued to a fixed date. These percentages indicate that those with shorter sentences tend to do their full time and do not get paroled, while as sentence length increases, there is a greater probability of being paroled.[21] Those with shorter sentences are less likely to be put in "limbo" (continued to a fixed date); as sentence length increases, individuals are more likely to be put in this category.

For the variable time served out of total sentence, coefficients are also high.

Those who have served 0 to 10 percent of their sentence have a 22 percent less likelihood of being paroled, and a 32 percent greater likelihood of being continued to a fixed date. Those who have served 11 to 30 percent of their sentence have a 5 percent greater likelihood of being continued to a fixed date. Those who have served 31 to 50 percent of their sentence have a 10 percent greater likelihood of being paroled and a 9 percent less likelihood of being continued to a fixed date. Those who have served 51 to 60 percent of their sentence have an 8 percent greater likelihood of being paroled, a 21 percent greater likelihood of being continued to expiration, and a 29 percent less likelihood of being continued to a fixed date. Those who have served over 60 percent of their time have a 6 percent greater likelihood of being paroled, a 23 percent greater likelihood of being continued to expiration, and a 29 percent less likelihood of being continued to a fixed date. In general, those who have served over 50 percent of their sentence are more likely to have to serve their full sentence if they have not been paroled by that time. One's likelihood of being paroled increases to the point where one has served up to 50 percent of one's sentence; after that, the likelihood of being paroled decreases.

Summing up, the independent predictor variables listed in Table 3-5 are shown to have some effect.[22]

Using the coefficients, one can obtain an estimated parole decision for each inmate in the sample. Table 3-6 indicates the relationship between the predicted parole decision and the actual parole decision.

In this case, 60.56 percent of those paroled were correctly classified; 69.38 percent of those continued to expiration were correctly classified; 78.92 percent of those continued to a fixed date were correctly classified. If we subtract from these the original proportions, we get an indication of how much we have improved over chance. This is indicated in Table 3-6. We have improved most for the category continued to expiration. We would have hoped to improve to a point close to 100 percent if these 27 factors are the ones actually being considered by the board in making its determinations.

The cumulative effects are not impressive relative to how well we do on the basis of chance alone. We do somewhat better than with the guidelines alone, but even with these 27 variables, much of the decision outcome remains unexplained. We can compare the Lambda obtained in our earlier analysis of the guidelines with the multivariate theta obtained through MNA. We convert the Lambda of 0.133 to a Theta score of 0.530.[23] This, when compared to the MNA multivariate theta of 0.712, indicates that we improve our explanatory and predictive power when we incorporate additional variables outside the scope of the guidelines.

In sum, the generalized R^2 of 38 percent indicates that two-thirds of the variance remains unexplained by the 27 predictor variables. The multivariate theta indicates that predictions have improved only 25 percent over chance. The bivariate eta squared and theta scores show the strongest relationship for the

Table 3-5
Effects of the 27 Predictor Variables

	Past		Present	Future
	Life History	Court	In Prison	
Variables that matter	Incarceration Age Offense Convictions	Sentence type Sentence length	Time served Prison punishment Custody classification Custody level reduced Job training	Living arrangement
Variables that do not matter	Codefendant Juvenile delinquent Marital status Race Parole revocation Grade claimed Employment Family criminal record Mental hospital confinement Homosexuality Military history Alcohol Drugs Car theft		Education	

Table 3-6
Classification Matrix

Actual		Paroled	Predicted Continued to Expiration	Continued to Fixed Date	
Paroled	N	1,265	381	443	2,089
	%	60.56	18.24	21.21	
Continued to Expiration	N	227	1,289	342	1,858
	%	12.22	69.38	18.41	
Continued to Fixed Date	N	475	229	2,635	3,339
	%	14.23	6.86	78.92	
		1,967	1,899	3,420	7,286

Proportion Correctly Classified:

		Paroled	Continued to Expiration	Continued to Fixed Date
	N	1,265	1,289	2,635
	%	60.56	69.38	78.92
Overall %		− 28.67	−25.50	−45.83
Improvement Over Chance		31.89	43.88	33.09

variables time served, length of sentence, and custody classification. Insofar as overall effect on the parole decision is concerned, length of sentence and time served are the most important factors. The guidelines, which emphasize the factor of time served, make explicit this interest of the board. This has also been noted with relationship to parole boards before:

Indications of rehabilitation, a lofty ideal, have never been the chief concern in determining a convict's sentence. Amount of time served for particular crimes has always been the primary factor, and the degree of variability of sentences because of indications of rehabilitation has always been very limited.[24]

The next chapter begins to analyze these statistical results in light of earlier discussion of particular cases that resulted in specific parole decisions, with the aim of understanding the board's practices in terms of the larger social and political context.

Appendix 3A:
NCCD Project and Parole
Decision Making

NCCD Parole Decision-Making Project

In 1970 a study was begun by the National Council on Crime and Delinquency (NCCD) Research Center at Davis, California, conducted in collaboration with the U.S. Board of Parole, and supported by a grant from the National Institute of Law Enforcement and Criminal Justice of the Law Enforcement Assistance Administration. A primary aim of this project was to "combine information items collected by various federal agencies about inmates and parolees into a data base suitable for computer-facilitated analyses of the relationships of information items to paroling decisions and to the consequences of those decisions."[1] The data base included information collected from the records of such agencies as the Bureau of Prisons, the U.S. Board of Parole, the Administrative Office of the United States Courts, and the Federal Bureau of Investigation. In general, the project was designed to explore the ways in which technological *hardware* (computer terminals) and *software* (statistical and other forms of informational analysis) might be used in the parole board's decision-making process. There was a felt need for summarizing the experience of the parole board to "improve" and increase the "effectiveness" of its decision-making process and provide it with a rational, "objective" base. It was hoped by this analysis of practice to make implicit paroling policies explicit and structure parole board discretion into uniform and consistent policy. The board would also be provided with a monitoring system to advise its members on the general trends in their decision-making policies and provide a means of testing for the congruence of actual and desired policy.

The researchers felt that models for procedures could be developed and made available in computerized form. The models were to be devised from information gathered on the background characteristics and past performance of inmates who appeared before the board during a two-year period, some of whom were paroled and some of whom were not. It was hoped that, ultimately, information on a potential parolee could be fed into the computer, which would then project an ideal, consistent, and fair release date, based upon the previously devised models. It was believed necessary to identify the weights given to various

The fact that the National Institute of Law Enforcement and Criminal Justice furnished financial support to the activity of the National Council On Crime and Delinquency relative to the Parole Decision-Making Project does not necessarily indicate the concurrence of the institute in the statements or conclusions described in the publications issued therefrom.

The fact that the U.S. Board of Parole collaborated with the National Council on Crime and Delinquency on the Parole Decision-Making Project does not necessarily indicate the concurrence of the board in the statements or conclusions that resulted therefrom.

63

factors representing statutory and board-defined criteria in the parole-selection process, and to measure relationships between various "offender attributes" to determine their effect on decision outcomes. This would provide a set of expected decisions for a given combination of factors that could be used as a way of maintaining consistency and rationality, and thereby "fairness."[2]

It was with these goals in mind that the National Council on Crime and Delinquency began to collect its data. The study population included all cases then being considered for parole by the board. A 50 percent sample of all persons considered for parole between November 1970 and November 1971 was chosen, and a 30 percent sample for the period November 1971 to June 1972. The sample-selection scheme was based on the five-digit individual identification number assigned to each inmate by the Bureau of Prisons. The 50 percent sample consisted of all cases whose last digit on the right was an odd number. The 30 percent sample was made up of all cases whose last digit was 1, 3, or 5. It was assumed that these procedures approximated random selection. The total sample consisted of 8,800 inmates.

The major task was to decide which factors in an inmate's life history were relevant to the decision to parole or not to parole. Items to be coded were selected from the code sheet of the Uniform Parole Reports (an NCCD follow-up study of parolees), from other parole studies, and from items available in the Bureau of Prisons files. Some items listed by the board as general factors determining parole selection were not collected and coded by the NCCD. It was pointed out that the nature of the case files used set limits upon the quality and type of data available to be extracted from them.[3]

The National Council on Crime and Delinquency gathered the following items of information:[4]

I.D. number; FBI number

Judicial district

Birthdate

Date probation began

Date sentence began

Date of admission

How committed

Type of admission

Sentence procedure

Expires full term

Mandatory release expected with good time

Minimum parole eligibility date

Aliases

Sex and ethnic group

Citizenship

Grade claimed

Marital status

Dependents

Codefendants

Type of sentence

Offense

Weapon in offense

Assault

Offense rating

Reason for first arrest

Age at first arrest

Age at first sentence

Age at first commitment

Longest time free since first commitment

Longest time served on any commitment

Prior prison commitments

Other prior sentences

Sentences with probation

Prior incarcerations

Probation or parole revocations

Prior arrests and convictions

Total arrests

Family criminal record

Living arrangement before commitment

Alcohol

Drugs

Mental hospital confinement

Homosexuality

Longest job in free community

Employment in last two years of civilian life

Military discharge

Beta IQ

SAT

Escape history

Prison adjustment indicated in first classification report

Custody classification prior to parole hearing

Custody level reduced during imprisonment

Assaultive infractions

Prison punishment

On-the-job training

Education program

Letters and visits from family

Number of parole hearings

Parole advisor obtained

Planned living arrangement

Type of decision

Decision outcome

Continued to date

Members

Date of decision

Projected release date

The NCCD tested its data for reliability[5] by giving the same data to two different coders and measuring the agreement between them. The number of cases used to measure reliability consisted of about one-tenth of the entire sample. Two different reliability samples were collected. As the study progressed, the coding manual was revised and improved as problems in definition were uncovered by the reliability measurement procedure. The coded items were divided into those that were continuous (where the coding was an actual number) and those that were categorical. Continuous variables were considered reliable if the correlation of the two codings was 0.80 or above. Items found to be unreliable were primarily related to prior convictions for some offenses, particularly sex offenses. The NCCD indicated that this was because these offenses rarely occur. Other errors were seen as due to overlap with other offenses or lack of clarity in the files, especially regarding juvenile delinquency. Out of 55 continuous items, 7 were considered unreliable. In our recoding procedures regarding offense, described in the next section, we probably eliminated many of the errors in offense coding by cross-tabulating offense rating with offense. For categorical items, the NCCD also used an arbitrary cut-off point of a coefficient of agreement of 0.80. There were 51 categorical items. In our study, some of the items found to be unreliable were not used. Several of the ones we did use were recombined and recoded and were probably more reliable, such as drug use. More problematic was employment in last two years before incarceration, for which there was seldom sufficient information in the case file, or which required computation by the coder. The NCCD noted, however, that this item was found to have predictive utility despite its relatively low reliability, because the distinction between "less than one year employment" and "unknown" and "less than 25 percent of the time" and "unknown" appeared to be unimportant. What was important was whether the subject was gainfully employed for any length of time, and this generally showed up in the file. Another important item shown to be unreliable was planned living arrangement, for which there was only sketchy information available. In recoding, recombining, and discarding cases that had missing information, we probably eliminated some of the error. Also, many of the items found to be unreliable were not used in our study. In sum, items that tended to be unreliable required either computation by the coder or was information that the case files did not record in any consistent or systematic fashion. We were unfortunately limited to dealing with the information the NCCD had chosen to gather.

The study by the National Council on Crime and Delinquency did not contain items dealing with certain criteria listed by the board, including the following:

Recommendations of the judge, United States attorney, probation department, caseworkers or other staff personnel

Results of psychiatric evaluations, data regarding attitudes toward self and others, changes in motivation and behavior, personal goals and strengths

Use of leisure time and recreation

Religion

Emotional health (other than mental hospital confinement or homosexuality)

Physical health

Therapy within the institution, kinds of educational programs or vocational training involved

Interpersonal relationships with staff and inmates

Employment and resources upon release

Results of scientific data and tools

Comments by hearing examiners

Many of the above are qualitative and would have required more elaborate coding procedures, while also allowing for greater potentiality of error. It is also possible that case files from which the information was taken did not contain the above data.

The most important uncollected information would appear to be that related to the inmate's future plans. The board stated in "You and the Parole Board," a pamphlet given to each inmate, that its ". . . primary interest is in your future, and the past is reviewed only as it is necessary or helpful in predicting what that future may be."[6] However, little information was gathered by the NCCD regarding the inmate's future. The only data they had was what the inmate's "planned living arrangement" was. It would appear that for them and for the board, the future was adequately indicated by this information. One might also maintain that "parole prognosis" or "salient-factor score" was in effect an indication of the inmate's future. But, this is essentially the future predetermined by the past, since only one of the nine salient factors relates to the future, and this is again whether the inmate plans to live with a spouse and/or child. This indicator is not relevant to whether the inmate will be able to sustain himself upon release. This would appear to be the most important missing information, the economic base from which a parolee must begin.[7] It would appear that, indeed, the inmate's past is the most important factor in granting parole. This is probably true if only for the fact that the greater part of the information available in the files relates to the past. The statement by the board, quoted above, is therefore misleading.

Recoded Analysis Variables

The following discussion of recoding refers only to those variables actually altered. Coding categories of variables retained as on the National Council on Crime and Delinquency Coding Sheets remain as indicated there.

It was necessary for us to recode some of the predictor variables to be able to use them in the multivariate nominal analysis. The following is a documentation of how this was done:

Age

The data from the NCCD gave the month and year of birth. To compute each individual's approximate age in years, the following formula was devised:

If year of birth was less than or equal to 57, Age = 1972 − (1900 + year of birth).[a]

If year of birth was greater than 57, Age = 1972 − (1800 + year of birth).

Individuals were then coded by age:

1 = Under 18 (these people were eliminated as too small a sample)

2 = 18-26

3 = 27-35

4 = 36 and over

Length of Sentence (in months)

The NCCD data included "date sentence began" and "date sentence expires," both in months and years. We used the following formula to determine length of sentence in months:

(date sentence expires − date sentence began)

(12 − month sentence began + month sentence expires) + ([year sentence expires − (year sentence began + 1901)] × 12)

The data was then coded as given in Table 3-3, variable 26.

Time Served Out of Total Sentence

First it was necessary to compute "time served." The NCCD data included "date sentence began" and "date of decision." The following formula was devised:

(date of decision − date sentence began)

---

[a]The NCCD data was gathered in 1972.

(12 − month sentence began + month of decision) + ([year of decision + 1900]
 − [year sentence began + 1901] × 12)

The ratio of time served out of length of sentence was computed from these two items, and coded as given in Table 3-3, variable 27.

Offense Severity

The data had been coded under two variables, "offense" and "offense rating." Offense refers to the crime for which the individual had been legally convicted and committed to prison. Offense rating was a qualitative interpretation of the behavior that resulted in commitment to prison.

Figure 3A-1 is a list of possible codes for both of these variables:

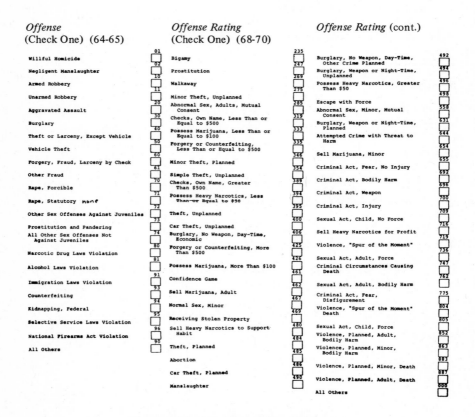

Figure 3A-1. Recoding Offense Severity

These two variables were combined into a single item, "offense severity," taken from the board's guidelines and their categorization of offenses. The categories of severity are:

1. Low
2. Low to moderate
3. Moderate
4. High
5. Very high
6. Greatest severity

We also generated a 7th code, which included those coded for both variables as "other." Individuals in this category ($N = 191$) were then eliminated from the analysis.

All of the offenses from the NCCD coding scheme were reclassified into the board's typology. First, "offense" was cross-tabulated with "offense rating" to obtain frequency distributions in the various categories. These were then grouped together according to the categories of severity in the guidelines.

Sentence Type

On the NCCD code sheet this variable is labeled "sentence precodure." The NCCD data included 21 codes for this variable, which were combined as follows:

1 = Regular adult and (a)(1) nos.

2 = Indeterminate — (a)(2) nos.

3 = All YCA (Youth Corrections Act) commitments

4 = All others

Parole Revocations

The NCCD study used four codes: none, probation revoked one or more times, parole revoked one or more times, both probation and parole revoked. The board's guidelines coded "parole revocation" as either Yes or No, and we also combined and coded in this way.

Total Convictions

Total convictions were coded by the NCCD in a series of offense-specific variables we summed up and combined into three categories. These are the same categories the board uses in its guidelines, as follows:

1 = No prior convictions

2 = 1 or 2 prior convictions

3 = 3 or more prior convictions

Total Incarcerations

The number of incarcerations was recorded on the NCCD code sheet ranging from 0 to 9. We recoded this item in the same way the board had done in its guidelines, which is the same coding scheme as for total convictions.

Juvenile Delinquency

Juvenile delinquency was taken from the NCCD variable "reason for first arrest," being the code category "delinquent child (under 18)." It was recoded as a dummy variable (Yes or No), as in the board's guidelines.

Race

Race was recoded as a dummy variable: nonwhite (black, Indian, other) and white.

Marital Status

Marital status was recoded to eliminate the categories "widower," which did not have enough cases, and "unknown," as missing data. These cases ($N = 120$) were eliminated, and the data recoded as given in Table 3-3, variable 8.

Grade Claimed

The NCCD data coded the variable grade-claimed on a continuum of grades completed in school, from 0 to 20. These were combined into three categories, listed in Table 3-3, variable 9. The board's guidelines include this as whether or not the individual has completed the 12th grade, as part of the "salient-factor score."

Military Discharge

Military discharge was recoded to combine general, medical, and honorable discharges.

Alcohol

Alcohol usage was recoded as a dummy variable, used or not used.

Drug Use

Use of drugs was coded by the NCCD as seven separate variables, which we combined into one, with codes as follows:

1 = No use

2 = Marijuana

3 = Heroin, cocaine, and barbiturates (combined together as the board has done in its guidelines)

4 = Other drugs

Custody Classification

The codes "maximum" and "close" were combined, as were "minimum" and "work release."

Education Program

"Yes" and "GED" were combined and recoded as follows:

0 = No or unknown

1 = Yes

Planned Living Arrangement

The category "with others" was recoded to include living with others in an institution or in the military. The two divisions of living alone, in a fixed abode or no fixed abode, were also combined as given in Table 3-3, variable 22.

Car Thief

This was taken from the NCCD variable "offense," using the code for vehicle theft. It was recoded as in the board's guidelines, as to whether the commitment offense included auto theft or not.

As previously pointed out, juveniles under 18 and women were eliminated, as these samples were too small. Cases that had unknown or missing data for the following variables were also eliminated: marital status, custody classification, offense, data sentence expires. Coding errors were also eliminated. These occurred in the coding of drug use, and there was one coding error in the dependent variable, parole decision. This brought our sample from the NCCD's 8,669 to 7,286.

Effects of Membership in Particular Categories of Predictor Variables on Parole Decision

Table 3A-1 illustrates the effects of membership in a particular category of an independent variable on the likelihood of being paroled or not. Effects are indicated by the coefficients listed in the table. (See also pages 57-60.)

Table 3A-1
Effects of Membership in Particular Categories of the 27 Predictor Variables on Parole Decision

	Paroled	Continued to Expiration	Continued to Fixed Date
1. Sentence type			
Regular adult (37.84%; N = 2,757)			
Percent	30.98	42.98	26.04
Coefficient	−0.14	1.98	−1.84
Adjusted percent	28.53	27.48	43.99
Indeterminate (31.55%; N = 2,299)			
Percent	21.53	20.57	57.89
Coefficient	−1.93	−2.98	4.91
Adjusted percent	26.74	22.52	50.74
YCA (22.39%; N = 1,631)			
Percent	34.58	5.89	59.53
Coefficient	2.53	2.82	−5.34
Adjusted percent	31.20	28.32	40.48
Other (8.22%; N = 599)			
Percent	29.38	17.36	53.26
Coefficient	1.17	−5.36	4.19
Adjusted percent	29.84	20.14	50.02
2. Codefendant			
No (47.38%; N = 3,452)			
Percent	27.14	29.46	43.40
Coefficient	−0.57	0.86	−0.29
Adjusted percent	28.10	26.36	45.54

	Paroled	Continued to Expiration	Continued to Fixed Date
Yes (52.62%; N = 3,834)			
Percent	30.05	21.94	48.02
Coefficient	0.51	−0.77	0.26
Adjusted percent	29.18	24.73	46.09
3. Parole revocations			
No (74.61%; N = 5,436)			
Percent	28.90	25.48	45.62
Coefficient	−0.04	0.09	−0.04
Adjusted percent	28.63	25.59	45.78
Yes (25.39%; N = 1,850)			
Percent	28.00	25.57	46.43
Coefficient	0.12	−0.25	0.13
Adjusted percent	28.79	25.25	45.96
4. Total convictions			
No prior convictions (0.03%; N = 2)			
Percent	50.00	0.00	50.00
Coefficient	−24.66	1.20	23.46
Adjusted percent	4.01	26.70	69.29
1 or 2 prior convictions (24.79%; N = 1,806)			
Percent	35.71	18.05	46.23
Coefficient	0.73	0.88	−1.61
Adjusted percent	29.40	26.38	44.22
3 or more prior convictions (75.19%; N = 5,478)			
Percent	26.34	27.97	45.69
Coefficient	−0.23	−0.29	0.52
Adjusted percent	28.44	25.21	46.35
5. Total incarcerations			
No prior incarcerations (33.85%; N = 2,466)			
Percent	36.90	17.15	45.94
Coefficient	5.53	−5.86	0.33
Adjusted percent	34.20	19.64	46.16
1 or 2 prior incarcerations (31.43%; N = 2,290)			
Percent	30.74	23.36	45.90
Coefficient	1.26	−2.19	0.93
Adjusted percent	29.93	23.31	46.76
3 or more prior incarcerations (34.72%; N = 2,530)			
Percent	18.77	35.57	45.65
Coefficient	−6.52	7.69	−1.17
Adjusted percent	22.15	33.19	44.66

Table 3A-1 (cont.)

	Paroled	Continued to Expiration	Continued to Fixed Date
6. Juvenile delinquent			
No (90.90%; N = 6,623)			
Percent	29.00	25.67	45.33
Coefficient	0.06	0.15	−0.21
Adjusted percent	28.73	25.65	45.62
Yes (9.10%; N = 663)			
Percent	25.34	23.83	50.83
Coefficient	−0.58	−1.49	2.07
Adjusted percent	28.09	24.01	47.90
7. Race			
Nonwhite (29.19%; N = 2,127)			
Percent	24.78	25.25	49.98
Coefficient	−1.92	1.32	0.59
Adjusted percent	26.76	26.82	46.42
White (70.81%; N = 5,159)			
Percent	30.28	25.61	44.12
Coefficient	0.79	−0.55	−0.24
Adjusted percent	29.46	24.96	45.58
8. Marital status			
Single (41.15%; N = 2,998)			
Percent	27.72	20.58	51.70
Coefficient	−1.35	0.09	1.26
Adjusted percent	27.32	25.59	47.08
Married (29.10%; N = 2,120)			
Percent	31.93	28.07	40.00
Coefficient	1.98	0.25	−2.23
Adjusted percent	30.66	25.75	43.60
Divorced (13.52%; N = 985)			
Percent	25.69	31.27	43.05
Coefficient	−1.90	0.95	0.95
Adjusted percent	26.77	26.45	46.78
Separated (11.84%; N = 863)			
Percent	27.46	29.43	43.11
Coefficient	0.97	−0.87	−0.10
Adjusted percent	29.64	24.63	45.73
Common-law (4.39%; N = 320)			
Percent	28.44	26.25	45.31
Coefficient	2.72	−3.08	0.36
Adjusted percent	31.39	22.42	46.19

	Paroled	Continued to Expiration	Continued to Fixed Date
9. Grade claimed			
Less than high school (66.73%; N = 4,862)			
Percent	26.35	27.33	46.32
Coefficient	−1.49	0.40	1.09
Adjusted percent	27.19	25.90	46.91
High school diploma (25.38%; N = 1,849)			
Percent	33.26	22.01	44.73
Coefficient	3.30	−0.57	−2.73
Adjusted percent	31.97	24.93	43.10
Higher education (7.89%; N = 575)			
Percent	33.57	21.22	45.22
Coefficient	1.95	−1.54	−0.40
Adjusted percent	30.62	23.96	45.42
10. Employment			
Verified employment for six months in last two years of civilian life, or student, or unemployable 75% of that time (51.30%; N = 3,738)			
Percent	33.09	23.27	43.63
Coefficient	1.83	−1.24	−0.59
Adjusted percent	30.50	24.26	45.24
Employed less than six months in last two years of civilian life, and not student or unemployable 75% of that time (13.70%; N = 998)			
Percent	24.45	26.05	49.50
Coefficient	−1.87	1.34	0.53
Adjusted percent	26.80	26.84	46.35
Employment not ascertained (35%; N = 2,550)			
Percent	23.84	28.55	47.61
Coefficient	−1.94	1.29	0.65
Adjusted percent	26.73	26.79	46.48
11. Family criminal record			
No (73.52%; N = 5,357)			
Percent	29.06	25.26	45.68
Coefficient	0.16	−0.08	−0.08
Adjusted percent	28.83	25.42	45.75
Yes (26.48%; N = 1,929)			
Percent	27.58	26.18	46.24
Coefficient	−0.44	0.21	0.23
Adjusted percent	28.23	25.71	46.05

Table 3A-1 (cont.)

	Paroled	Continued to Expiration	Continued to Fixed Date
12. Mental hospital			
No (91.55%; N = 6,670)			
Percent	29.16	25.50	45.34
Coefficient	0.06	0.10	−0.17
Adjusted percent	28.74	25.60	45.66
Yes (8.45%; N = 616)			
Percent	23.38	25.49	51.14
Coefficient	−0.69	−1.11	1.80
Adjusted percent	27.98	24.39	47.63
13. Homosexuality			
No (96.09%; N = 7,001)			
Percent	28.94	25.55	45.51
Coefficient	0.10	0.04	−0.14
Adjusted percent	28.77	25.54	45.69
Yes (3.91%; N = 285)			
Percent	22.11	24.21	53.68
Coefficient	−2.49	−0.90	3.39
Adjusted percent	26.18	24.60	49.21
14. Military discharge			
No military history (61.39%; N = 4,473)			
Percent	27.83	25.22	46.95
Coefficient	−0.30	0.78	−0.48
Adjusted percent	28.37	26.28	45.35
Honorable discharge (21.97%; N = 1,601)			
Percent	31.36	26.30	42.35
Coefficient	1.09	−2.17	1.08
Adjusted percent	29.76	23.33	46.91
Other than honorable discharge (13.15%; N = 958)			
Percent	26.62	28.29	45.09
Coefficient	−1.34	0.97	0.37
Adjusted percent	27.33	26.47	46.19
Other (3.49%; N = 254)			
Percent	34.25	14.96	50.79
Coefficient	3.50	−3.81	0.31
Adjusted percent	32.17	21.69	46.14
15. Alcohol			
No use (42.55%; N = 3,100)			
Percent	29.71	23.71	46.58
Coefficient	0.55	−0.75	0.20
Adjusted percent	29.22	24.75	46.03

	Paroled	Continued to Expiration	Continued to Fixed Date
Use (57.45%; N = 4,186)			
Percent	27.90	26.83	45.27
Coefficient	−0.40	0.56	−0.15
Adjusted percent	28.27	26.06	45.68
16. Drug use			
No use (63.63%; N = 4,636)			
Percent	30.52	28.39	41.09
Coefficient	0.63	−0.46	−0.17
Adjusted percent	29.30	25.04	45.65
Marijuana (21.56%; N = 1,571)			
Percent	26.86	17.76	55.38
Coefficient	−1.40	1.92	−0.52
Adjusted percent	27.27	27.42	45.30
Heroin, cocaine, or barbiturates (11.60%; N = 845)			
Percent	22.96	25.68	51.36
Coefficient	−0.63	0.32	0.31
Adjusted percent	28.04	25.82	46.14
Other (3.21%; N = 234)			
Percent	24.79	19.66	55.56
Coefficient	−0.84	−5.01	5.86
Adjusted percent	27.83	20.49	51.69
17. Custody classification			
Maximum (31.97%; N = 2,329)			
Percent	10.48	23.01	66.51
Coefficient	−11.86	6.38	5.48
Adjusted percent	16.81	31.88	51.31
Medium (32.13%; N = 2,341)			
Percent	22.21	27.64	50.15
Coefficient	−5.07	2.09	2.98
Adjusted percent	23.61	27.59	48.81
Minimum (35.90%; N = 2,616)			
Percent	50.65	25.80	23.55
Coefficient	15.09	−7.55	−7.54
Adjusted percent	43.76	17.95	38.28
18. Custody level reduced			
No (74.84%; N = 5,453)			
Percent	20.19	28.24	51.57
Coefficient	−1.82	−0.62	2.45
Adjusted percent	26.85	24.88	48.27

Table 3A-1 (cont.)

	Paroled	Continued to Expiration	Continued to Fixed Date
Yes (25.16%; N = 1,833)			
Percent	53.90	17.35	28.75
Coefficient	5.42	1.86	−7.28
Adjusted percent	34.09	27.36	38.55
19. Job training			
None or unknown (71.60%; N = 5,217)			
Percent	22.89	29.65	47.46
Coefficient	−2.30	0.86	1.44
Adjusted percent	26.37	26.36	47.27
Less than or equal to five months (11.36%; N = 828)			
Percent	22.34	20.89	56.76
Coefficient	−5.05	1.02	4.03
Adjusted percent	23.62	26.52	49.86
More than five months (17.03%; N = 1,241)			
Percent	57.21	11.12	31.67
Coefficient	13.03	−4.28	−8.75
Adjusted percent	41.70	21.22	37.08
20. Education program			
No or unknown (57.04%; N = 4,156)			
Percent	22.06	31.42	46.51
Coefficient	−1.79	0.78	1.02
Adjusted percent	26.88	26.28	46.84
Yes (42.96%; N = 3,130)			
Percent	37.44	17.64	44.92
Coefficient	2.38	−1.03	−1.35
Adjusted percent	31.05	24.47	44.48
21. Prison punishment			
No (77.35%; N = 5,636)			
Percent	27.89	26.05	46.06
Coefficient	2.23	−1.09	−1.15
Adjusted percent	30.90	24.42	44.68
Yes (22.65%; N = 1,650)			
Percent	31.33	23.64	45.03
Coefficient	−7.62	3.71	3.92
Adjusted percent	21.05	29.21	49.74
22. Planned living arrangement			
With parents or guardian (32.45%; N = 2,364)			
Percent	33.93	22.50	43.57
Coefficient	2.99	−0.18	−2.81
Adjusted percent	31.66	25.32	43.01

	Paroled	Continued to Expiration	Continued to Fixed Date
With wife and/or children (24.40%; N = 1,778)			
Percent	30.88	29.30	39.82
Coefficient	−0.17	−2.88	3.05
Adjusted percent	28.50	22.62	48.87
With paramour (4.50%; N = 328)			
Percent	19.21	32.01	48.78
Coefficient	−4.23	1.68	2.55
Adjusted percent	24.44	27.18	48.38
With others (16.84%; N = 1,227)			
Percent	33.09	26.65	40.26
Coefficient	2.85	0.05	−3.35
Adjusted percent	31.53	26.00	42.48
Alone (8.07%; N = 588)			
Percent	34.69	27.38	37.93
Coefficient	3.40	−0.34	−3.05
Adjusted percent	32.07	25.16	42.77
No plans (13.74%; N = 1,001)			
Percent	6.49	21.18	72.33
Coefficient	−10.87	4.57	6.30
Adjusted percent	17.80	30.07	52.13
23. Offense severity			
Low severity (1.95%; N = 142)			
Percent	16.20	64.79	19.01
Coefficient	0.60	4.72	−5.32
Adjusted percent	29.27	30.22	40.51
Low to moderate severity (14.42%; N = 1,051)			
Percent	34.44	33.30	32.25
Coefficient	3.73	−1.30	−2.43
Adjusted percent	32.40	24.20	43.40
Moderate severity (23.29%; N = 1,697)			
Percent	29.17	25.52	45.32
Coefficient	2.78	−3.29	0.51
Adjusted percent	31.45	22.21	46.33
High severity (42.04%; N = 3,063)			
Percent	29.09	26.31	44.60
Coefficient	−0.41	0.06	0.35
Adjusted percent	28.26	25.56	46.17
Very high severity (16.90%; N = 1,231)			
Percent	23.07	13.40	63.53
Coefficient	−6.13	4.62	1.51
Adjusted percent	22.54	30.12	47.34

Table 3A-1 (cont.)

	Paroled	*Continued to Expiration*	*Continued to Fixed Date*
Greatest severity (1.4%; *N* = 102)			
Percent	33.33	11.76	54.90
Coefficient	0.75	3.89	−4.65
Adjusted percent	29.43	29.39	41.18
24. Car thief			
No (74.76%; *N* = 5,447)			
Percent	28.25	24.64	47.11
Coefficient	0.07	−0.44	0.37
Adjusted percent	28.74	25.06	46.20
Yes (25.24%; *N* = 1,839)			
Percent	29.91	28.06	42.03
Coefficient	−0.20	1.30	−1.10
Adjusted percent	28.47	26.80	44.73
25. Age			
18-26 (42.11%; *N* = 3,068)			
Percent	29.99	15.35	54.66
Coefficient	2.47	−6.31	3.84
Adjusted percent	31.14	19.19	49.67
27-35 (30.33%; *N* = 2,210)			
Percent	27.87	31.00	41.13
Coefficient	−0.51	2.95	−2.44
Adjusted percent	28.16	28.45	43.39
36 and over (27.56%; *N* = 2,008)			
Percent	27.54	34.96	37.50
Coefficient	−3.21	6.40	−3.19
Adjusted percent	25.46	31.90	42.64
26. Length of sentence			
Up to 12 months (7.01%; *N* = 511)			
Percent	17.61	81.41	0.98
Coefficient	−24.14	60.97	−36.83
Adjusted percent	4.53	86.47	8.99
13-24 months (13.72%; *N* = 1,000)			
Percent	25.00	57.60	17.40
Coefficient	−11.07	36.50	−25.43
Adjusted percent	17.60	62.00	20.40
25-36 months (15.41%; *N* = 1,123)			
Percent	28.50	28.41	43.10
Coefficient	−5.46	5.59	−0.13
Adjusted percent	23.21	31.09	45.70

	Paroled	Continued to Expiration	Continued to Fixed Date
37-48 months (6.9%; $N = 503$)			
Percent	25.84	22.86	51.29
Coefficient	−3.41	−2.35	5.76
Adjusted percent	25.26	23.15	51.59
49-60 months (13.33%; $N = 971$)			
Percent	28.63	18.33	53.04
Coefficient	1.81	−8.09	6.28
Adjusted percent	30.49	17.41	52.11
61-120 months (34.07%; $N = 2,482$)			
Percent	33.24	8.62	58.14
Coefficient	8.26	−17.38	9.12
Adjusted percent	36.93	8.12	54.95
121-180 months (5.11%; $N = 372$)			
Percent	27.42	6.72	65.86
Coefficient	11.19	−29.10	17.91
Adjusted percent	39.86	−3.60	63.73
181 months and over (4.45%; $N = 324$)			
Percent	29.01	4.63	66.36
Coefficient	14.88	−33.69	18.81
Adjusted percent	43.55	−8.19	64.64
27. Time served out of total sentence			
0-10% (17.95%; $N = 1,308$)			
Percent	2.06	1.07	96.87
Coefficient	−22.30	−9.81	32.11
Adjusted percent	6.38	15.69	77.93
11-30% (33.54%; $N = 2,444$)			
Percent	27.91	24.55	47.55
Coefficient	−0.49	−4.70	5.19
Adjusted percent	28.19	20.80	51.02
31-50% (32.65%; $N = 2,379$)			
Percent	38.92	31.53	29.55
Coefficient	9.54	−0.41	−9.13
Adjusted percent	38.21	25.09	36.70
51-60% (7.14%; $N = 520$)			
Percent	38.08	45.58	16.35
Coefficient	7.94	20.59	−28.53
Adjusted percent	36.61	46.09	17.30
61% and over (8.72%; $N = 635$)			
Percent	40.31	40.47	19.21
Coefficient	5.56	22.98	−28.54
Adjusted percent	34.24	48.48	17.29

Note: N = Number of cases.

84

Parole Decision in the Cases of Arthur Young, Robert Green, and Bill Gardner

The following documents pertaining to the cases of Young, Green, and Gardner illustrate further the nature of parole decision making and use of the guidelines.

Parole Form 11-7
(Rev. May, 1976)

UNITED STATES DEPARTMENT OF JUSTICE
United States Parole Commission
Washington, D. C. 20537

Notice of Action

Name ___Arthur Young___

Register Number _____ *Institution* Terminal Island

In the case of the above-named the following action with regard to parole, parole status, or mandatory release was ordered:

Continue to Expiration with an Interim Progress Report in May, 1975.

(Reasons for continuance or revocation) (Conditions or remarks)

Your offense behavior has been rated as very high severity. You have a salient factor score of 9. You have been in custody a total of 7 months. Guidelines established by the Board for adult cases which consider the above factors indicate a range of 26-36 mos. to be served before release for cases with good institutional program performance and adjustment. After careful consideration of all relevant factors and information presented, it is found that a decision outside the guidelines at this consideration does not appear warranted.

Appeals procedure: You have a right to appeal a decision as shown below. Filing the appeal is your responsibility which others cannot perform for you. Forms for that purpose may be obtained from your caseworker, or the Regional Office of the Commission, and must be filed with the Commission within thirty days of the date this Notice was sent.

A. Decision of a Hearing Examiner Panel. Appeal may be made to the Regional Commissioner
B. Decision of the National Commissioners when referred to them for reconsideration. Appeal may be made to the Regional Commissioner.
C. Decision of the Regional Commissioner. Appeal may be made to the National Appeals Board.
D. Decision of National Commissioners in cases where they assumed original jurisdiction. Appeal may be made to the entire Commission.
E. Decision of a Regional Commissioner relative to Parole condition or continuance under supervision. Appeal may be made to the National Appeals Board.

Copies of this notice are sent to your institution and/or your probation officer. In certain cases copies may also be sent to the sentencing court. You are responsible for advising any others to whom you might wish to make information on this form available.

November 1, 1974 NAB
(Date Notice sent)   (Region) (NAB) (Nat. Dir)   (Docket Clerk)

INMATE COPY   FPI LC 6-76 848C 8KT8 8471

Date __April 1975__

UNITED STATES DEPARTMENT OF JUSTICE
BUREAU OF PRISONS
FEDERAL CORRECTIONAL INSTITUTION
TERMINAL ISLAND, CALIFORNIA

Inmate Reviewed and/or Received Copy

_____

SIGNATURE AND DATE

_____

PROGRESS REPORT

IRH_____Interim___X_____Annual_____Other_____

Name:_Young, Arthur_____Reg. No.:_____

Offense:_Distribution of Narcotics S-2 (Cocaine)_____Age:___35_____

Sentence:_3 yrs. 4208 (a)(2)_____Began:_9-23-74___Months Served:___12_____

Days EGT:___38_____Days FGT:___0_____Tentative Release:___6-22-76_____

Last Board Action and Date:_Continue to expiration with interim Progress Report May 1975;_
November 1, 1974

Detainers:__None_____

_____

Codefendants: James Johnson, 2 yrs. FCI T.I. plus three years Special Parole Term; Tim
Tracy, nine months (to serve three months and six months suspended), two
years probation and three years Special Parole Term to follow.

_____

NEW INFORMATION

The only new information is that Young's business is now closed down, but he plans to reopen the business upon release. Young states that his wife is presently living in Montreal,
Canada and that she will rejoin him upon his release. There is no other significant new information.

INSTITUTIONAL ADJUSTMENT

Young was originally classified on May 31, 1974 and at that time goals of upgrading his
educational level and voluntary groups were established. Young has been participating in the

Adult Basic Education class in order to raise his grade level. He has also participated in two outside college classes—the Human Relations class and the English class. All reports indicate that he is progressing in excellent fashion in the Education Department. He has been actively participating in the Jaycees Program and has received several furloughs in order to attend Jaycee meetings outside the institution. He has participated on these furloughs without any incident. Because of his sewing skills, Young was assigned to the Clothing Room. His job supervisor reports that he has been the custodian of the inmate "hot room." He states that he is very capable of getting along with personnel and seeing that they are fitted with proper clothing. He further states that Young has saved the institution quite a bit of money because of his knowledge of sewing machines and work saving devices. He states that he is very mature in his attitude toward authority and that he has progressed in bettering himself for his release to society. His housing officer reports that he gets along well with others, that he keeps himself and his area very neat. He states that he seems to avoid speaking to staff members, but when he does he is polite and respectful. The Catholic Chaplain states that Young actively participates in the Catholic religious program. He further adds that he is a volunteer member of the chapel choir. The Recreation Supervisor reports that Young is a very active person in lifting weights, playing handball, and playing basketball. The Chief Medical Officer reports that his general health is good and that he has no disabilities. There is nothing indicated in the way of physical defect that would adversely effect his employability. Young has made excellent institutional adjustment, having received no incident reports or adverse comments. All comments in his jacket have been positive. Due to good adjustment he was awarded minimum custody. In summary, Young has made excellent adjustment to Terminal Island and is in the process of completing all goals.

RELEASE PLANNING

Furloughs have been used in this case in order to help provide Young a transition into the community. They will also be used in the future. Community programs, such as Work or Study Release will be used in the future in order to prepare Young for his release. Young plans to reopen his sewing contractor business when he is released into the community. He states that his lawyer is in the process of getting back a sum of money for him that was seized with his business. If this does not materialize, Young has other job skills as a mechanic, a welder, and a sewing machine repairman. Pre-release counseling will be employed in this case in order to develop a strong release plan. He plans to reunite with his wife in Los Angeles, California upon release.

Release Plans:

A. Residence: Young owns a home in Los Angeles, California and will live there with his wife.

B. Employer: He plans to reopen a Sewing Contractors business in Los Angeles. If this does not materialize, Young will seek employment in other fields for which he has skills.

C. Advisor: Request U.S. Probation Officer to act in this capacity.

D. USPO Los Angeles, California

EVALUATION AND RECOMMENDATION FOR RELEASE

In April of 1975 Young will have served 12 months on his three year (a)(2) sentence. Young has been making excellent progress at completing the goals established for him at his original classification. He has been participating in education courses, and the Jaycees. He has participated on several furloughs and has made excellent adjustment. He has received no incident reports at Terminal Island and all the comments in his file are positive. It is felt that Young can benefit from further programming and that he can benefit from Work or Study Release in the future. Young has the skills and intelligence to adjust to society without violating the law at this time. However, his offense is extremely serious and sophisticated. The Case Management Team concurs that Young would make a good parole candidate in the future, but due to the seriousness of his offense, will not make a recommendation at this time.

Dictate by: Case Manager

January 24, 1975

Mr. Victor Sherman
8383 Wilshire Boulevard
Beverly Hills, California 90211

Re: Robert Green

Dear Mr. Sherman:

I have represented Robert Green, an inmate at La Tuna Federal Correctional Institution, in his efforts to obtain his release on parole.

Mr. Green was arrested on November 22, 1972 and charged with possession of marijuana with intent to distribute. On November 30, 1973, he pled guilty to one count of conspiracy to smuggle 305 pounds of marijuana and was sentenced under the provisions of Title 21 U.S.C.S. § 4208 (a) (2) to five years imprisonment and five years special parole. A copy of said judgment and commitment is enclosed.

On June 16, 1973, after having been at La Tuna three months, Mr. Green appeared before the Parole Board but was advised that in his particular case, the panel before which he was appearing would make no recommendation either for or against his possible parole and that it would be left completely up to the Board of Parole in Washington, D.C.

My client was given a twenty-eight month set-off which meant that he would reappear before the Parole Board in December 1975.

Mr. Green and his wife spent months contacting various officials trying to ascertain why he had received such a long set-off. No answers were ever given to them. At this point, Mr. & Mrs. Green retained me to aid them in getting some of the answers to their questions and if possible in helping obtain his parole.

Eventually a new Parole Board hearing was given to Mr. Green based on the fact that a twenty-eight month set-off was contrary to the then existing rules of parole which stated that a prisoner could only be given a maximum of a twenty-four month set-off.

On October 12, 1974, accompanied by myself, Mr. Green met with the Parole Board for the second time. At this hearing the Parole Board members, applying the guidelines set out in the new Federal Guidelines for Parole and Probation, placed Mr. Green in the "very good" category of the Defendant characteristics with salient-factor score of nine points. However, the examiners then went on to state that because of the conspiratorial nature of the crime involved they were going to, "in this particular case," consider marijuana a soft drug and place it in the "very high" severity category, thus making the recommended time to be served twenty-six to thirty-six months instead of sixteen to twenty months normally recommended to be served by those involved in smuggling marijuana. The Board interestingly enough then proceeded to state that because of his "exceptional institutional behavior" he would be paroled on December 19, 1974 one month and three days before the guidelines would have allowed if the "very high" category were in fact correct. At the time both Mr. Green and myself were fully satisfied with the whole outcome in spite of the fact that the Parole Board had arbitrarily decided that for this particular case it would consider marijuana a "soft drug" and completely ignore the fact that the guidelines plainly showed "marijuana" in quantities over $5,000.00 to be placed in the "high" category.

Based on the fact that the Parole Board gave Mr. Green a release date of December 19, 1974, Mrs. Green proceeded to vacate their apartment here in El Paso, Texas, sell all of their furnishings and moved to San Diego, California, in accordance with the parole release plan. On November 4, 1974, Mr. Green was notified that the Regional Director had referred his parole decision to the National Appellate Board for reconsideration, a copy of the notice is enclosed. On November 12, 1974, Mr. Green received notification that the National Appellate Board had denied him parole on December 19, 1974 based on the fact that nothing they could see warranted his release outside the guidelines. He was given a Parole Board hearing for August, 1975. A copy of the Appellate Board decision is also enclosed.

The Appellate Board decision was appealed under § 2.24 of the guidelines but was as expected, rejected by the Regional Director to whom the appeal was directed.

After a great deal of effort Mr. Green was able to obtain a transfer to Terminal Island where all concerned agree he has a better chance of getting a fair hearing on a Writ of Habeas Corpus.

I am sure that if Mr. Green's case gets a fair and impartial hearing he will be released immediately. I personally do not understand the reason why the government has gone to such extremes to block this man's release, especially since all the others convicted with Mr. Green have been paroled. The only thing I can think of is that he is a pilot and was arrested once before for a similar charge which was dismissed after the evidence was suppressed.

You should have received a retainer of $1,000.00 by this time but if you have not, please contact my office and I will make sure you do. Please proceed with this matter with all possible speed and keep me informed on all developments.

Very truly yours,

Robert R. Harris

RRH:dm
Enclosures

Robert Green
Parole Hearing
Oct. 12, 1974

Williams: Mr. Green, my name is Williams. I'm a representative of Mr. Johnson, the Board of Examiners who will conduct your review hearing today. You have attorney Robert Harris here acting as your representative. We have already explained to you the general procedure. You will be allowed to make a statement at the end of the hearing. We ask that it be brief and to the point to say what you feel. Mr. Green, you have received notice that you would have your hearing this week, is that true?

Green: Yes.

W: And you have decided to have Mr. Harris act as your representative?

G: Yes, sir.

W: You have hired him to do this or is he appearing as a personal friend?

G: Both.

W: How long have you known Mr. Harris?

G: Oh, about four or five months.

W: OK. Now the offense you're here for involved how much marijuana?

G: There's a little bit _____ about it but it said on the indictment 305 pounds and another 355. So I really don't know; there were a hundred and some odd packages of it.

W: And you at that time were involved as I understand it as a middle man and as a pilot.

G: No sir, there wasn't any flying involved in this at all.

G: Well, I was arrested in Arizona on a deal, but again there was no plane involved.

W: What were you accused of?

G: I was accused of conspiracy, possession for distribution.

W: When you were committed for this offense you had a pending charge.

G: No sir the charges had already been dismissed.

W: OK. I'm looking at the picture here. Did you at one time _____ shave your head bald?

G: When I came in here they'd had a rash of lice in the county jail so they shaved me when I came in here.

W: The picture needs to be updated I would assume looking at it _____ OK. Now you today have been in this institution for 23 months.

G: Yes, sir.

W: Let's go over the _____ fact. Let me mention that we'll be giving you our decision at the end of today's hearing. Our decision will be tentative, the formal decision will come to you by way of a notice of action. We'll have reasons on it if our decision is not in your favor. Our decision may be changed, it's not likely, but it may be subject to review. If you desire to appeal an adverse decision you may do so during the 30-day period starting with the date of the notice of action. Then you for that purpose _____ forms to be made available to you by the case worker. OK? Now, I note that you have had two convictions, one is rather ancient but you have had two prior convictions, right?

G: No, one prior conviction.

W: OK, let's clarify that. In 1952, this is the ancient one, were you not convicted of drunk driving.

G: No, sir, I was not.

W: Who was that? Were you in Wichita, Kansas at all during 1952?

G: Oh, yes. I don't believe I was convicted on that.

W: They have that you were fined $101.90 and given a 90-day _____ that probably was suspended if you don't remember. However, you were convicted in 1966 of striking an officer in the face and received a three-month suspended sentence.

G: May I clarify that a little bit.

W: Go right ahead.

G: That striking an officer sounds pretty bad. What had happened on that was a group of men and I rented a boat in San Diego and on our way back in to San Diego the captain had been drinking quite a bit and I got into a little bit of an altercation with him and what would have normally been just an assault, I guess, turned out to be pretty bad because it happened with the captain of a boat on the high seas.

W: Then the officer was the captain of the boat?

G: He was the captain of the boat, yes, sir.

W: You have had no prior incarcerations? Employment _____ down to employment and we can't verify any employment.

G Well, I've been self-employed almost all of my life. Was raised in the cattle business and then my father, when he died, he left my brother and I and sister a ranch and we've been in that business, well, for as long as I can remember.

W: And do you turn in tax forms every year?

G: Well the ranch is in Mexico. He bought this ranch in the 1930's in Mexico.

W: Did you claim any income for the purpose of United States tax purposes?

G: To the best of my knowledge, the information I've been able to get, unless you earn over $18,000 a year you don't have to. My brother and I are both in this situation that we're pretty much familiar with.

W: Did you reside in the United States?

G: No, sir, I lived most of my life in Mexico.

W: OK. We cannot consider that verified employment. That's just an area where we have no verification. However, that doesn't affect _____ bracket in terms of your total score, your total score is 9 out of a possible 11 points so this leaves you in a very good category. For the purpose of classifying the offense _____ we've classified it as very high. So you're _____ right in the guidelines in the 26 to 36 bracket.

G: Could you clarify that for me please, sir?

W: The circumstances of the offense indicate the sale of soft drugs in excess of $5,000 _____

G: Does that put me into the high category?

W: It puts you in the very high category. Under drugs in the very high category . . . soft drugs, sale, more than $5,000.

G: _____ $5,000 or more _____ up in the high category.

W: That soft drug, sale, $5,000; marijuana, $5,000 or more; marijuana is a soft drug which is a very high classification too.

G: So, where does it fit then?

W: We're placing it in the very high. Behavior, the conspiracy _____ everything in our evaluation indicates that this is a very high offense. If that is an area you wish to contend you may do so _____ the appeal procedure. To date, within this institution, you've made an excellent institutional adjustment. Now you've worked as a dental assistant what does that mean?

G: I assist him in his work up there in oral surgery and all types of dental work, filling, orthodontic work, prosthetics, false teeth. I make part of them. Help to fit them, assist doing surgery. It's a rather complicated job but I've had a lot of fun doing this.

W: _____ on reports doing it too. Now for release, you have vacillated between two different areas and you now have acceptance for a plan in San Diego.

G: Yes, sir. The reason for that being that my mother _____ and wife's people all live in San Diego. My wife's mother has been extremely sick all during this year and seems to be getting worse as time is going by. She would like to get out there and spend a little time with her plus I'd like to get out of El Paso. I've met everybody in the world here. I'd just like to get out there and start clean. Don't want to get back into the same El Paso merry-go-round.

W: OK, you will work as a dry wall installer. Would that satisfy you?

G: No . . . basically I'm going to wind up running a crew for this man. A lot of his employees are green card employees who don't speak any Spanish and I've had experience in the construction business and I think I can fit in pretty well as a foreman due to the fact that I am bilingual and I am familiar with the construction business.

W: All right, Mr. Johnson _____ Mr. Harris?

Harris: Sir, I would first like to point out that in the high category, you've got marijuana, sale, $5,000.00 or more. And right below that, the very line below that you've got soft drugs, possession, $5,000 or more. Clearly they don't mean marijuana and soft drugs as the same thing. Why would they be so repetitive. It's obvious that when they mean marijuana they say marijuana. And if _____ talk about marijuana they say that drug's marijuana. They would not call the same drug twice by two different names in the same category. Obviously what they're talking about when they talk about soft drugs is they're not heroin, cocaine and that sort of thing. They would be talking about barbiturates and that type of thing. This man clearly fits into the high category. There have been over 40 or 50 other people who have come through with the same exact charge and they have never been told that theirs were particularly going to be classified soft instead of marijuana. Now obviously, this thing . . .

W: We'll note your feelings, sir. I'm not going to argue with you . . .

H: I don't exactly understand what _____ they've got against this man but clearly what might categorize . . .

W: Let me state it's not the institution that makes the classification. The institution might look at this and try to determine what they feel we will assess it as, however, we're the ones that do that.

H: Marijuana is marijuana. And I don't understand why it was classified as a different drug in this case. It was marijuana. There is no reason whatsoever other than that he's put into a different category. This wasn't even a particularly large amount of marijuana. There are people in here who have gotten out in 16 to 20 who have been caught for having a ton of marijuana or two tons of marijuana. And this man, I don't know what exactly _____ I'm sure that he is _____ because he insists on coming up before the board and I don't think that's fair to take that and hold it against him and have him in this institution unnecessarily long.

W: I assume he had been rescheduled for hearing. I meant to cover the story here and I did not, because of communications before. We have not received any communication that's _____ to the institution to indicate why the case was reopened. All we know _____ asked to reconsider.

H: _____ new parole board hearing. Slight difference and I don't see, it's my understanding that if the person is going to be under or over the guidelines there's got to be an exception and there's got to be certain reasons for it. _____ give reasons why it should be over and I don't see how this man has been _____ in some cases would say that if a man for example has been charged with possession of stolen materials and he is sentenced in _____ category the board knows that actually this man stole the material and he used a gun, he threatened people's lives to do it, he was only convicted for stealing. They know that it was actually armed robbery. In that case they can raise it to the next category but in this case there is no such information that there was an armed robbery involved. Nothing of the sort. There was a small amount of marijuana to be quite honest. There is no reason _____ this man does not fit into any reason why there should be an exception. I don't _____ in the whole time he's been here.

W: Mr. Harris, Mr. Harris, you're starting to repeat yourself. We have taken what you've said; would you go on to your next point please.

H: Well, there's not much point in going on because I realize in that category he automatically gets _____ . I hope that my comments don't prejudice you against Mr. Green. He didn't have any idea that I was going to say this but I didn't have any idea that you were going to put him in a different category so _____ I hope you don't take my personal feelings and _____ what's gotten involved here into this thing. And my personal view that I hope you don't _____ . . .

W: Mr. Harris, what you said just now, it automatically results in a 26 month set-off. Now if you will read _____ . . .

H: Unintelligible.

W: I gave you a chance, now give me a chance. If you will read that you will find that that is not an expression—set-off. It is an expression of time to be served under normal circumstances. Now if we were to follow the guidelines today we would not set Mr. Green off 26 to 36 months. What we're talking about is a matter of a three-month set-off _____ follow the guidelines.

H: Again, I hope you don't take my personal disappointment _____ . . .

W: What we are doing with your remarks is taking the facts from the statements you make. Your emotions . . . that's your own self. Assuming that the man, Mr. Green, had been classified _____ what comments would you make to that?

H: Only to go over that what he was planning on saying. Some of his background. My personal view is that the man has been a perfect gentleman. I've met his wife and his family and they're all good people. I realize this man got himself into some trouble. He's 43 years old and he'd like to start clean. He's got every opportunity to never return to this place and he's got every reason to never return. He's well educated, has a good background, comes from a good family. He got himself into . . . I understand . . . greed. It does strange things to different people. I think he's over that. He realizes now he's not trying to set the world on fire financially and all he wants to do now is get out of prison, make a home for himself and his wife. He's got two adopted children now and he'd like to help raise them. That's it. Thank you.

W: Mr. Green, is there anything else?

G: One thing, I talked to Mr. (unintelligible), my caseworker when I signed a progress report and there were a couple of pieces of information there that weren't correct and he said to bring them up at this time. _____ the date of birth is wrong, I was born on December 7th, 1930 and not December 30th, 1930. I am the fourth of four children, not the second of three. And there is information in there that my wife died in _____ from an overdose of narcotics and this is not true. She died of a combination of barbiturates and alcohol . . . we'd been out partying and she came back and took some sleeping pills and the combination killed her. Both for reasons of this Board and for personal reasons I wanted to clarify that because she was a fine girl. I've had a good institutional record here. I've had minimum custody since September of 1973. I've been out on eight or nine town trips with absolute minimum security. Mr. Bird took me out on several of them where we were just completely turned loose. I have a front gate pass in connection with my work in the dental clinic and also in connection with my work as a photographer for the JC's. I have a side gate pass and have a roof pass in connection with my volunteer work as a prison projectionist. I have been submitted for 30 days extra good time for this work. I have had excellent recommendations from the staff members and get along with them well. I've had no disciplinary action of any kind since I've been in here. I went to work in the dental clinic three days after I came to this institution. I went up and got the job myself. It was something that I had always been interested in and I decided I would do my best to try and get into it and learn something about it and I work steadily there. It's hard work. It's complicated and so it takes quite a while to learn. I have also had an excellent recommendation for extra good time from the hospital for my assistance in emergencies up there, one in particular. The good time wasn't granted me, it didn't fall in the category of a section 9, but it is an excellent report. I've lived in the honor block for about 14 months now or 15 months and have never had any problems in there of any kind and like Mr. . . . .

W: Let me tell you we've read all of this in the reports that what you're emphasizing is your excellent institutional adjustment.

G: I'm very happily married and I have a good job that I'm going to like and I'm going to enjoy this job to go to. (long blank spot on tape) I realize that I did a lot of wrong both legally and in the sense that I've damaged my family, all of my family, not only my wife. All of my nieces, nephews, brother and sister. And I think more than anything that this has been good for me to be in here. It's changed my sense of values. Before I used to think a lot about money, possessions, things like this and this has made me realize how important family and friends are. I'd like to get out of here, get a good job, get a home established with my wife. I'm 43, going on 44 years old and it's about time I started thinking about settling down and looking to the future. I was indicted with five other people, six codefendants in all in this case. Four of those codefendants have already been released, one though dismissal of charges and three by _____ parole. And other than that just give me all the breaks you can.

W: Would you step outside?

G: Yes, sir.

W: _____ very high. The effect itself, $20,000 is significant _____ $5,000 plus your behavior during the time indicates that you were pretty deeply involved. At any rate, utilizing the adult guidelines your release bracket would start during January of 75. Do you calculate that too?

G: Well, in effect I'm in the 26th month to you sir?

W: Alright. You've done well here and for that reason we're going to go under the guidelines just a little bit and we're going to give you a parole date of December 19th. That'll get you home for Christmas and it'll give you time to prepare things.

G: That's fine . . . beautiful. Thank you very much.

W: Now, let me remind you that there's a lot of smoke in your case. You know it.

G: I know that I came into this place with a bad reputation and the only way I can live that reputation down is just not doing that again.

W: You never get arrested again, your reputation will never bother you.

G: I've been down hard, I know. I've got five years special parole on top of that. I think I'm going to be a pretty good guy.

W: Alright, if you'll give me a signature here. This is a review hearing in the case of Robert Green, number _____ during the hearing period. It should be noted regarding the assessment that the attorney remarked strongly that high rather than very high. _____ attempt to distribute marijuana and to date including jail time he has served a total of 23 months _____

Parole Form H-7
(Rev. May, 1976)

UNITED STATES DEPARTMENT OF JUSTICE
United States Parole Commission
Washington, D. C. 20537

Notice of Action

Name Robert Green

Register Number _____ *Institution* La Tuna

In the case of the above-named the following action with regard to parole, parole status, or mandatory release was ordered:

Referred to the National Appellate Board for Reconsideration of the Hearing Panel's Decision.

(Reasons for continuance or revocation) (Conditions or remarks)

Subject advised 11/4/74 -- George Reed

Oct. 29, 1974   South Central – NAB
(Date Notice sent)   (Region) (NAB) (Nat. Dir)   (Docket Clerk)

INMATE COPY

98

Parole Form H-7
(Rev. May, 1976)

UNITED STATES DEPARTMENT OF JUSTICE
United States Parole Commission
Washington, D. C. 20537
—AMENDED—
Notice of Action

Name   Robert Green

Register Number _____ *Institution* Terminal Island

In the case of the above-named the following action with regard to parole, parole status, or mandatory release was ordered:

Continue with an Institutional Review Hearing, August, 1975.

(Reasons for continuance or revocation) (Conditions or remarks)

Your offense behavior has been rated as very high severity. You have a salient factor score of 9. Guidelines established by the Board which consider the above factors indicate a range of 26-36 months to be served before release for adult cases with good institutional program performance and adjustment. You have been in custody a total of 23 months. After careful consideration of all relevant factors and information presented, it is found that a decision outside the guidelines at this consideration does not appear warranted. There is not a reasonable probability that you would live and remain at liberty without violating the law. Your offense falls in the "very high" severity category because you were the ringleader of a very serious commercial marihuana venture.

Appeals procedure: You have a right to appeal a decision as shown below. Filing the appeal is your responsibility which others cannot perform for you. Forms for that purpose may be obtained from your caseworker, or the Regional Office of the Commission, and must be filed with the Commission within thirty days of the date this Notice was sent.

A. Decision of a Hearing Examiner Panel. Appeal may be made to the Regional Commissioner.
B. Decision of the National Commissioners when referred to them for reconsideration. Appeal may be made to the Regional Commissioner.
C. Decision of the Regional Commissioner. Appeal may be made to the National Appeals Board.
D. Decision of National Commissioners in cases where they assumed original jurisdiction. Appeal may be made to the entire Commission.
E. Decision of a Regional Commissioner relative to Parole condition or continuance under supervision. Appeal may be made to the National Appeals Board.

Copies of this notice are sent to your institution and/or your probation officer. In certain cases copies may also be sent to the sentencing court. You are responsible for advising any others to whom you might wish to make information on this form available.

March 12, 1975   South Central
(Date Notice sent)   (Region) (NAB) (Nat. Dir)   (Docket Clerk)

INMATE COPY   FPI LC 6-76 84SC SETS 9471

UNITED STATES COURT OF APPEALS
FOR THE NINTH CIRCUIT

ROBERT GREEN,)

        Appellant,)

     v.)   O R D E R

MAURICE H. SIGLER, Chairman)
UNITED STATES BOARD OF PAROLE,)
UNITED BUREAU OF PRISONS,)

        Appellees.)

_____)

Before: ELY and CHOY, Circuit Judges, and SOLOMON,
          District Judge.*

    The appellant's Motion for release on bail, pending the disposition of the subject appeal, is hereby granted.

    It is ordered that the Federal Correctional Institution at Terminal Island, California forthwith release Green upon a condition that Green deposit $10.00 in cash bail with the Clerk of the District Court for the Central District of California.

/S/ Walter Ely
_____

/S/ Herbert Y.C. Choy
_____

United States Circuit Judges

_____

United States District Judge

---

*Honorable Gus J. Solomon, Senior United States District Judge, Portland, Oregon, sitting by designation.

Bill Gardner
"F" Unit
Lompoc, California 93436

March 11, 1974

Youth Division
United States Board of Parole
HOLC Building
101 Indiana Avenue, N.W.
Washington, D.C. 20537

Attention: Mr. Daniel J. Capodanno
Case Analyst

Dear Mr. Capodanno:

Thank you for your letter of February 1 advising me of the alternatives available for obtaining a re-hearing of my case with the Board of Parole.

Before I elaborate on my reasons for wanting a reconsideration in my case, I want to make it clear that I do not expect to be parolled immediately or even in the near future. I am aware of my culpability and accountability for the crime I committed. I know that I must pay for what I did, but the degree of my punishment is what I question at this time.

In the 90-day waiting period since the last official action, I have explored the possibilities of the suggestions you made in your last letter to me. I contacted my caseworker about a possible review and re-opening of my case, but since he has been a caseworker for only a very short time, he said that he was not familiar enough with my case to take any action at present. I understand this and am therefore going to follow your second suggestion in submitting relevant information and supporting materials directly to your office. I have also contacted my attorney about a possible in-person review hearing, but in light of the upcoming regionalization of the Board, we felt that it would be more efficient to wait until this might be necessary.

Perhaps the most important and significant fact in determining my possible parole eligibility which I felt was overlooked at the time of my institutional review hearing is the fact that I was living in the free community for nearly eighteen months after the time of my arrest. During this time, I moved to an entirely new environment and successfully readjusted and reorganized my life from what it was before I was arrested. My purpose was not to depreciate or forget about the serious trouble I was in, but was more of an attempt to reinstitute myself into a respectable way of life. My record in this community was exemplary of a good citizen and there are letters from people in the community to support my claim. Please note that one of the letters is from Mr. Dennis Haynes, Chief of Police of Ketchum (population approximately 1,000), who is familiar with me and knows me as a law-abiding citizen. I have my own business in this community and employment will be no problem.

Another factor which I feel should be brought up at this time is my amended sentence computation record which was corrected after my institutional review hearing. Changes which are significant are: #15; change to "non-narcotics S-1", offenses 963, 960, 841; and #16; BOP Offense Code change to 382. Before these changes were made, clerical errors had me down as a second offender in narcotics. Exactly the opposite is true—this is my first conviction, first time in jail, first arrest, and my crime involves hashish, a marijuana derivitive. (15 kg.) I had no criminal record whatsoever before the time of my arrest, and in the two years since my arrest (6 months of this time here at Lompoc), I have not had an infraction of any kind.

The next piece of significant information which I would like to draw your attention to is my Program Plan which was made up after my initial classification here at Lompoc. In Sections B and E, develop work habits and redirect association with the drug environment, please be advised that I have held the same job since I arrived at the institution. I am the secretary to the Superintendent of Federal Prison Industries, a job which I feel makes more than the ordinary demands of an institutional job. My work record is outstanding and I was awarded first grade pay within three months after being hired. My association with the drug environment ended long before I ever came to this institution. I admit that I have smoked marijuana and hashish in the past, but I have not indulged in any drug usage whatsoever in over eighteen months. Drugs got me into trouble in the first place, so for me, it is merely common sense that induced me to leave that experimentation behind me forever. None of my friends in Idaho use drugs and I feel that it is safe to say that any association I ever had with a drug environment is buried in my past. The only association I now have to contend with in terms of drugs is right here in the institution. This is no place to redirect an association with an environment, since so many of the people here are in for drug related crimes.

My only referral here at the institution was to the Peer Counseling Program. I have completed this program in courses in Transactional Analysis and Structure and Dynamics. I have also completed a course in Remotivation offered by the 7th Step Foundation. I can program no further in this institution since I have completed all but one course necessary for a baccalaureate degree in English and Philosophy at the University of the Pacific in Stockton, California.

Last, and perhaps most important in this request for a rehearing, is the fact that with the extra good time which I am earning and will continue to earn by working at Industries, my tentative release date will be moved up to April 4, 1976. Since I do not go back to the Board until November, 1975, this puts my tentative parole date and tentative expiration date very close together. I feel that the Board saw no reason for having me continue to expiration or else they would have done so. As it was at the time of my hearing, I was given a chance to be released approximately nine months ahead of my expiration date. I feel that at this time, in light of my institution record thusfar, that I should still have the advantage of the possibility of being paroled at a time considerably less than my expiration date. I feel that it is at least fair to ask that I be given a chance to go back to the board after 1/3 of my sentence. I have an A-2 sentence, but as it is now, I will be doing more time than if I had a Regular Adult sentence and maintained the same institution record.

It has been two years since I committed my crime and though this may not seem like very much time to you, in my mind, considering the changes I have undertaken in improving my own life, this has been a long time. I have accomplished much in rehabilitating and restructuring my life and I feel that this should be taken into consideration in reconsidering my parole status. A prolonged incarceration will do little more than alienate me from what I have done to improve myself. If I have to do two more years in jail, I will be no better off than I was two years ago. Again, I will have to face the monumental task of restructuring and reorganizing my life. This is indeed punishment, but society as well as the individual is being punished.

On the basis of the information contained in this letter and enclosures, I pray that the parole board will see fit to make a reconsideration in my case.

Sincerely,

Bill Gardner

Enclosures (13)

Bill Gardner
Post Office Box W
Lompoc, California 93436

April 1, 1974

Youth Division
United States Board of Parole
HOLC Building
101 Indiana Ave, N.W.
Washington, D.C. 20537

Attention: Mr. Daniel J. Capodanno
          Case Analyst

Dear Mr. Capodanno:

In reference to my letter to you of March 11, 1974, I wish to inform you that I have been in touch with my caseworker and the Chief of Case Management, Mr. Edman, regarding the discrepancies I noted on page 2 of my letter. It has been discovered that not only was my sentence computation sheet in error, but my Pre-sentence report as well. Somehow, my sentences for 21-963, 960(a)(1), and 841(a)(1) were interpreted as narcotic violations instead of non-narcotic S-1.

With this erroneous information, my record reflects that I could have possibly received a sentence up to 35 years. The fact of the matter is that the maximum sentence for my crime could have amounted to 5 years, but that I received a 4 year A-2 sentence.

I will be meeting with my caseworker again today and will try to initiate the steps necessary to have my record corrected. A letter corroborating what I have stated in this letter should be coming to Washington from my caseworker shortly.

Please add the information contained within this letter to my letter of March 11, 1974. Thank you again for your consideration of this matter.

                                        Sincerely,

                                        Bill Gardner

Parole Form H-7
(Rev. May, 1976)

UNITED STATES DEPARTMENT OF JUSTICE
United States Parole Commission
Washington, D. C. 20537

Notice of Action

Name   Bill Gardner

Register Number _____ *Institution* _____
                        A LC

In the case of the above-named the following action with regard to parole, parole status, or mandatory release was ordered:

CONTINUE WITH AN IRH IN NOVEMBER 1975

(Reasons for continuance or revocation) (Conditions or remarks)

Appeals procedure: You have a right to appeal a decision as shown below. Filing the appeal is your responsibility which others cannot perform for you. Forms for that purpose may be obtained from your caseworker, or the Regional Office of the Commission, and must be filed wit the Commission within thirty days of the date this Notice was sent.

A. Decision of a Hearing Examiner Panel. Appeal may be made to the Regional Commissioner.

B. Decision of the National Commissioners when referred to them for reconsideration. Appeal may be made to the Regional Commissioner.

C. Decision of the Regional Commissioner. Appeal may be made to the National Appeals Board.

D. Decision of National Commissioners in cases where they assumed original jurisdiction. Appeal may be made to the entire Commission.

E. Decision of a Regional Commissioner relative to Parole condition or continuance under supervision. Appeal may be made to the National Appeals Board.

Copies of this notice are sent to your institution and/or your probation officer. In certain cases copies may also be sent to the sentencing court. You are responsible for advising any others to whom you might wish to make information on this form available.

Nov. 30, 1973
(Date Notice sent)   (Region) (NAB) (Nat. Dir)   (Docket Clerk)

INMATE COPY

FPI LC 6-76 84SC SETS 9471

Parole Form H 7
(Rev. May, 1976)

UNITED STATES DEPARTMENT OF JUSTICE
United States Parole Commission
Washington, D. C. 20537

Notice of Action

Name _____Bill Gardner_____

Register Number _____ ____ *Institution* _Lompoc_

In the case of the above-named the following action with regard to parole, parole status, or mandatory release was ordered:

Reopen and continue for IRH November 1975 with interim Progress Report in March 1975.

(Reasons for continuance or revocation) (Conditions or remarks)

Appeals procedure: You have a right to appeal a decision as shown below. Filing the appeal is your responsibility which others cannot perform for you. Forms for that purpose may be obtained from your caseworker, or the Regional Office of the Commission, and must be filed with the Commission within thirty days of the date this Notice was sent.

A. Decision of a Hearing Examiner Panel. Appeal may be made to the Regional Commissioner.
B. Decision of the National Commissioners when referred to them for reconsideration. Appeal may be made to the Regional Commissioner.
C. Decision of the Regional Commissioner. Appeal may be made to the National Appeals Board.
D. Decision of National Commissioners in cases where they assumed original jurisdiction. Appeal may be made to the entire Commission.
E. Decision of a Regional Commissioner relative to Parole condition or continuance under supervision. Appeal may be made to the National Appeals Board.

Copies of this notice are sent to your institution and/or your probation officer. In certain cases copies may also be sent to the sentencing court. You are responsible for advising any others to whom you might wish to make information on this form available.

January 27, 1975   Western
(Date Notice sent)   (Region) (NAB) (Nat. Dir)   (Docket Clerk)

INMATE COPY

FPI LC 8-76 84SC SETS 9471

DATE: <u>January 28, 1975</u>

UNITED STATES DEPARTMENT OF JUSTICE
BUREAU OF PRISONS

<u>FPC, Lompoc, California</u>
INSTITUTION

Inmate Reviewed and/or <u>Received</u> Copy

_____

Signature and Date

PROGRESS REPORT

IRH_____ Interim __XX_____ Annual_____ Other_____

Name: _Gardner, Bill_____ Reg No:_____

Offense: _Distribution of Non Narcotic S-1_____ Age:__28_____

Sentence: _4 Yrs 4208 (a)(2)___ Began:__7-25-72_____ Months Served:___19___
            With 3 Yrs SPT   (24 Days Jail Time)

Days FGT:__62__ Days FGT:___00__ Tentative Release:____4-29-76_____

Last Board Action and Date: _____

_____

Detainers:__None._____

_____

Codefendants:_Jim King, Fugitive. Gardner indicates the U.S. Attorney declined to prose-

cute in this case._____

NEW INFORMATION

No new information.

BP-Class-2
(Rev. 11/74)

Page 2_____

UNITED STATES DEPARTMENT OF JUSTICE
BUREAU OF PRISONS
FPC, LOMPOC, CALIFORNIA
PROGRESS REPORT
(Continued)

Committed Name Gardner, Bill   Date   01-28-75

INSTITUTIONAL ADJUSTMENT

Gardner was transferred to Lompoc Camp on December 26, 1974. He is making an above average response to confinement at this facility, but it is actually too soon to evaluate, as he has only been here a short time. Gardner was not programmed for educational or vocational activities at this facility. However, he has been assigned to the Meat Processing VT and from all indications, it can be assumed that he will complete this program by March, 1975. His supervisor indicates Gardner is performing above average and that he relates well with others on the job. While at the main institution, Gardner states he did complete the Heating and Air-Conditioning vocational program and has received an MDTA Certificate for completion of the Two-Way Street Program. In spite of the two incident reports, it is felt Gardner has made an excellent response to confinement and has participated in several self improvement programs. His conduct record has remained clear at the Camp. He has not participated in community programs to this date, but will be evaluated for furlough in the near future. In his leisure time, he studies meat cutting lessons in the evenings from several books, plays bridge and takes part in creative writing. He is in good physical and mental health at this time and would be employable.

RELEASE PLANNING

Upon release Gardner anticipates relocation to Ventura, California. He will reunite with his common-law wife upon release and anticipates employment with Buena Ventura Academy in Ventura. The BVA is a home for retarded children.

Release Plans: As indicated above, Gardner anticipates residing with his common-law wife, and should have a verified offer of employment in the file when this report is reviewed. As of the date of this report, there is no verified offer of employment, however, Gardner indicates his common-law wife has made several contacts with the work supervisors. His common-law wife also is employed at BVA.

A.   Residence—Ms Sue Abbott (Common-law wife) Ventura, California.

B.   Employer—Director, Buena Ventura Academy, Ventura Blvd., Ventura, California.

C.   Advisor—none.

D.   USPO—R. Latta, Chief, Los Angeles, California.

EVALUATION AND RECOMMENDATION FOR RELEASE

In spite of the severity of the instant offense, our staff believes Gardner has the ability to remain in the community without violating the law. The classification team recommends parole to the above plan.

Dictated by: _____
                          Senior Case Manager

MV:cc

NOTICE OF ACTION – PART II – SALIENT FACTORS

Case Name BILL GARDNER   Register Number _____

Item A   2

    No prior convictions (adult or juvenile) = 2
    One or two prior convictions = 1
    Three or more prior convictions = 0

Item B   2

    No prior incacerations (adult or juvenile) = 2
    One or two prior incacerations = 1
    Three or more prior incacerations = 0

Item C   1

    Age at first commitment (adult or juvenile) 18 years or older = 1
    Otherwise = 0

Item D   1

    Commitment offense did not involve auto theft = 1
    Otherwise = 0

Item E   1

    Never had parole revoked or been committed for a new offense while
      on parole = 1
    Otherwise = 0

Item F   1

    No history of heroin, cocaine, or barbiturate dependence = 1
    Otherwise = 0

Item G   1

    Has completed 12th grade or received GED = 1
    Otherwise = 0

Item H   1

    Verified employment (or full-time school attendance) for a total
      of at least 6 months during the last 2 years in the community = 1
    Otherwise = 0

Item I   1

    Release plan to live with spouse and/or children = 1
    Otherwise = 0

Total Score   11

February 7, 1975

Mr. Robert Vogler
Post Office Box W
Lompoc, Calif. 93436

Dear Mr. Vogler:

This afternoon I received a rather anxious letter from Bill Gardner. It seems that a Special Progress Report is due to be submitted on Monday, February 10 on behalf of Mr. Gardner. Although I understand that the report does recommend that he be granted parole, the report also contains a serious error regarding the charges for which he was convicted— namely that the offense was a "narcotic" offense rather than one involving a non-narcotic substance. I am sure that the error is a mere oversight on someone's part; however, it is one that can, as you may well imagine, greatly damage Mr. Gardner's chances for being granted parole in March of this year. Although the Justice Department's Sentence Computation Record was corrected in November of 1973 (see attached copy enclosed herein), the Attorney General's office apparently neglected to also rectify the misinformation in the U.S. Attorney's Report (Form 89).

I spoke with Mr. Darrell MacIntyre, the Assistant U.S. Attorney who prosecuted Mr. Gardner, and he is now aware of the error, and is taking the steps required to rectify it. He also promised to telephone you on Monday, February 10, so that you may be personally informed of the change that needs to be made in Mr. Gardner's SPR, and can proceed with correcting the mistake immediately, so that Mr. Gardner's chances for parole are neither hindered nor delayed.

Both Mr. Gardner and myself will greatly appreciate prompt action on this matter, as it would be extremely unfair for Mr. Gardner to be further penalized because of a clerical error.

Very truly yours,

Michael D. Nasatir

MDN/sg
cc: Mr. Darrell MacIntyre
    Bill Gardner

Parole Form H-7
(Rev. May, 1976)

UNITED STATES DEPARTMENT OF JUSTICE
United States Parole Commission
Washington, D. C. 20537

Notice of Action

Name _____ Bill Gardner _____

Register Number _____ *Institution* <u>Lompoc</u>
Camp

In the case of the above-named the following action with regard to parole, parole status, or mandatory release was ordered:

No change in previous Board Order dated January 27, 1975.

(Reasons for continuance or revocation) (Conditions or remarks)

No new information significant enough to change previous decision.

Appeals procedure: You have a right to appeal a decision as shown below. Filing the appeal is your responsibility which others cannot perform for you. Forms for that purpose may be obtained from your caseworker, or the Regional Office of the Commission, and must be filed with the Commission within thirty days of the date this Notice was sent.

A. Decision of a Hearing Examiner Panel. Appeal may be made to the Regional Commissioner.
B. Decision of the National Commissioners when referred to them for reconsideration. Appeal may be made to the Regional Commissioner.
C. Decision of the Regional Commissioner. Appeal may be made to the National Appeals Board.
D. Decision of National Commissioners in cases where they assumed original jurisdiction. Appeal may be made to the entire Commission.
E. Decision of a Regional Commissioner relative to Parole condition or continuance under supervision. Appeal may be made to the National Appeals Board.

Copies of this notice are sent to your institution and/or your probation officer. In certain cases copies may also be sent to the sentencing court. You are responsible for advising any others to whom you might wish to make information on this form available.

March 13, 1975   Western
(Date Notice sent)   (Region) (NAB) (Nat. Dir)   (Docket Clerk)

INMATE COPY   FPI LC 6-76 64SC SETS 9471

4

The Political Economy of Parole

They take a city girl and put her in prison and she picks tomatoes for four years—it's oblivion—and then they send her back to the city as "socially adjusted." I was so "adjusted" that even the bus ride back to Philadelphia scared the s--t out of me—the noise and the people talking and moving around. I just shut my eyes and prayed to survive the trip.

Women in Prison

How, then, shall we begin to make sense of the process of parole? What is it that differentiates those who are paroled from those who are not? What is the essential nature of parole guidelines and the decision-making process? Will an analysis of these questions lead us to an understanding of parole within the broader social structure?

Such questions cannot be answered by statistical means, although we have used statistics to help us. Our quantitative analysis has indicated that certain factors that are supposed to have an effect on parole decisions do not in fact have an effect. Erik Wright, a student chaplain at San Quentin for nine months, was allowed to sit in on some parole board sessions.[1] He noted that the most discussion and weight was given to the inmate's disciplinary record. Prisoners recognized this, and pointed out to him that how hard you worked on your job or in school did not seem to matter very much. Another important theme pervading parole board hearings was whether the prisoner felt remorse for his crime. Those who did not were assumed to "need more time to think things over." Perhaps these issues are some of the undisclosed criteria that neither the parole board nor criminologists have specified, and that may have been operating in the empirical study described in Chapter 3. The NCCD did not gather data on such variables. Most criminologists who studied parole never sat in on actual parole board hearings.[2] In the tradition of positivism, many of them took for granted what the parole board said its criteria were and began their research from there. There was little questioning of the reality as defined by the board. In order not to repeat the same error, we must continue our analysis in another way, and get beneath the level of appearances or ideology to the level of social reality. We propose to use the method of dialectical materialism[3] to do this, and base our analysis on the political economy of imprisonment and parole.

111

Prison and Politics

It has been accepted as given that "under modern concepts of penology, paroling prisoners is part of the rehabilitory aim of the correctional philosophy. The objective is to return a prisoner to a full family and community life."[4] We must begin to question this basic assumption, for the actual practice of imprisonment and parole does not support it. Studies have shown that prisons are not environments where "rehabilitation" can take place. Prisons are not places where people can, for example, learn job skills that do not lead to dead-end, menial, low-paying jobs outside prison.[5] Many studies have shown that there are few rehabilitative opportunities in prisons and that "corrections" has failed. Such studies have been ignored, however, and prisons have not changed. We can find in prisons an analogy to schools. The current criticism directed towards schools is that they have failed, that they are dysfunctional, that they are not doing what they are supposed to do. Just the opposite is true—schools are and have been doing exactly what they were intended to do: produce the labor power and reproduce social relations as they exist between the working force and those who own their labor power. The rhetoric was simply ideological. The ideologies of education and individual success function to keep working-class parents and youths convinced that it is up to them to make it up the ladder through education. Education, however, maintains class divisions and keeps people in their places.[6]

Prisons have functioned in a similar way. Prisons are institutions set up to perform a service for capitalist society, and that is the exclusion and elimination of particular groups of people who threaten the system. The process is legitimated by a network of ideas, which provides the ideological fortress supporting the actual physical structure. The concept of parole and its attendant myths of "readiness" and "prognosis for success," are basic elements of this ideological frame. Other social scientists have come to the same conclusion.

So the question one obviously asks is what does the machine produce, what is that gigantic installation used for and what comes out of it. At the time of the Auburn and of the Philadelphia prison which served as models (with rather little change until now) for the great machines of incarceration, it was believed that something indeed was produced: "virtuous" men. Now we know, and the administration is perfectly aware, that no such thing is produced. That nothing at all is produced. That it's a question simply of a great trick of sleight of hand, a curious mechanism of circular elimination: Society eliminates by sending to prison people whom prison breaks up, crushes, physically eliminates; and then once they have been broken up, the prison eliminates them by "freeing" them and sending them back to society; and there, their life in prison, the way in which they were treated, the state in which they come out, insures that society will eliminate them once again, sending them to prison which in turn . . .[7]

Prisons and parole were never designed to return people to their family and community better able and equipped to maintain their existence, but, rather, to eliminate the "dangerous classes." Prison is not only punitive, it is part of an eliminative process. "Prison is the physical elimination of people who come out of it, who die of it sometimes directly, and almost always indirectly insofar as they can no longer find a trade, don't have anything to live on, cannot reconstitute a family any more, etc., and finally passing from one prison to another or from one crime to another end up by actually being physically eliminated."[8] From this perspective, parole is part of the exercise and maintenance of power by the ruling class and a tool in the class struggle. "Rehabilitation" must be a myth and an impossibility when we recognize that the economic system cannot provide jobs for people who are not in prison, much less for an additional 1.5 million parolees.

Over 1 million prisoners and parolees form a large part of the industrial reserve army of labor. Under capitalism, there is always a surplus population for whom there is no work. This reserve labor force serves to keep wages of the working class in check so that surplus value and accumulation of wealth by the capitalists can continue.

But if a surplus laboring population is a necessary product of accumulation or of the development of wealth on a capitalist basis, this surplus population becomes, conversely, the level of capitalist accumulation, nay, a condition of existence of the capitalist mode of production. It forms an industrial reserve army that belongs to capital quite as absolutely as if the latter had bred it at its own cost. Independently of the limits of the actual increase of population, it creates for the changing needs of the self-expansion of capital a mass of human material always ready for exploitation.[9]

The capitalist labor force consists of two parts, the employed and the unemployed, with part-time workers somewhere in between. All categories of workers expand or contract as technology changes, as the business cycle goes through its ups and downs, and along with the vagaries of the market, all part of capitalist production.

The industrial reserve army, during the periods of stagnation and average prosperity, weighs down the active labor army; during the periods of overproduction and paroxysm, it holds its pretensions in check. Relative surplus population is therefore the pivot upon which the law of demand and supply of labor works.[10]

The amount of "criminality" corresponds to the amount of unemployment, the fluctuating size of the reserve labor force.[11] It was recently reported that "crime" jumped 18 percent in the first three months of 1975 over the same period a year ago,[12] and this was during a period of high unemployment. A recent study by the U.S. Bureau of Prisons showed an important correlation between unemployment and increases in the federal prison population. The bureau pointed out that, "When unemployment of males 20 and over goes up or down, the population of the Federal Prison System usually follows the same pattern allowing for a time lag of 15 months."[13] Fifteen months was found to be the best time lag to describe the process between arrest, trial, conviction, and eventual confinement. Figure 4-1 is a copy of their graph indicating the correlation between Bureau of Prisons inmate population matched with the unemployment index from 15 months earlier. The first quarter unemployment index for males over 20 was matched with the bureau's population figure 15 months later. This match was made for each year-end population figure from 1952 through 1974. The correlation computed from these figures was 0.77, a result that could be expected by chance alone less than one time in a thousand. The Bureau of Prisons hopes to use these figures for an indication of population trends more than a year in advance to tailor its budgetary, building, and operational plans accordingly. The aim is greater social control and practical policy, rather than theoretical understanding of why people need to commit crimes and/or an attempt to find work for people who are unemployed.

The finding of a relationship between crime and "poverty" is not new. As E. Sutherland and D. Cressey point out, "Studies of the economic status of criminals have indicated that the lower economic class has a much higher official crime rate than the upper economic class."[14] For example, in three series of "offenders" studied by S. and E. Glueck,[15] 71.3 percent juvenile delinquents,

Source: U.S. Bureau of Prisons Report, March 1975.

Figure 4-1. Bureau of Prisons Inmate Population Matched with Unemployment Index from 15 Months Earlier

71.2 percent young-adult males, and 91.3 percent women were below the "comfortable level," which was defined as possession of sufficient surplus to enable a family to maintain itself for four months without going on relief. Despite similar findings in many studies,[16] the correlation between social class and criminal activity has been minimized. In part, this is because white-collar criminality is widespread (but not prosecuted). Sutherland pointed out, "When white-collar crimes are taken into account, however, they throw doubt on the conclusion that crime is concentrated in the lower economic classes."[17] While there is undoubtedly a great deal of white-collar crime, it is not really treated as "crime," and does not have the same consequences. Therefore, what does constitute "crime" *is* lower class activity. Official definitions of crime are what matter when only certain classes of people are being treated as criminals and processed through the court system and sent to prison.

A recent survey of 141,600 inmates of local jails in 1972, the "first nationwide attempt to assess the socioeconomic characteristics of the country's jail population,"[18] is a rare instance where data on the variable "annual income" was gathered. Generally, statistical surveys of prisoners gather data on age, race, sex, types of offenses, and time served, but omit data pertaining to social class.[19] The National Council on Crime and Delinquency data used here did include information on employment of prisoners, but this was broadly defined as "employment in last two years of civilian life," which could be coded as (a) more than 25 percent of the time or student or unemployable 75 percent of the time, (b) less than 26 percent of the time and not student or unemployable 75 percent of the time, or (c) unknown. This does not indicate the "occupation" of the inmates, their "annual income," or whether they worked part or full time.[20]

The annual income level of inmates found in the Survey of Inmates of Local Jails is indicated in Table 4-1. During the year preceding their admission to jail, almost half of the inmates earned an income below that defined by the United States government as poverty level for persons without dependents. About two out of every five were unemployed at the time of admission, and roughly 20 percent of those employed were part-time workers only.[21] More than 55 percent of the inmates in local jails throughout the United States were awaiting trial or were in one of the other stages of being processed by the courts. It is extremely interesting that at the three lower levels, differences between the races disappear, and that prearrest annual incomes for all levels except $7,500 or more are very close for blacks and whites. One might say that inmates of jails are likely to be poorer than inmates of state and federal prisons because those in jail are to a great extent those who cannot make bail. However, it was pointed out that one-fourth of the jail inmates had been denied bail because of the "seriousness" of their crime. Second, studies have shown that persons out on bail stand a much better chance of receiving a favorable disposition of their case and not going to prison.[22] Thus, we would expect the annual income of jail inmates to be similar to the annual income of prison inmates.

Table 4-1
Selected Socioeconomic Characteristics of Jail Inmates, by Race

	All Races		White		Black		Other	
				Race				
Characteristic	Number	Percent	Number	Percent	Number	Percent	Number	Percent
Prearrest annual income								
Less than $2,000	51,800	44	33,500	42	26,800	46	1,600	58
$2,000-$2,999	16,100	11	8,600	11	7,000	12	400	14
$3,000-$7,499	44,400	31	24,800	31	19,000	32	600	22
$7,500 or more	15,100	11	10,800	14	4,300	7	a	a
Not available	4,300	3	2,200	3	2,000	3	a	a

Source: U.S. Department of Justice, Law Enforcement Assistance Administration, *Survey of Inmates of Local Jails, 1972.*

Note: Detail may not add to totals because of rounding.

aLess than 300 inmates

Erik Wright also pointed out that prisons are disproportionately filled with the poor and uneducated.

Forty-one percent of the general labor force falls into white-collar employment categories (clerical and sales, managers and owners, and professional and technical workers), compared to only 14 percent of the prison population. At the other extreme, 43 percent of the prisoners are manual laborers or service workers, compared to only 17 percent of the total labor force. The same pattern is found for education: 55 percent of the prisoners have an elementary school education or less, compared to only 34 percent of the general population; 45 percent of the general population are high school graduates compared to only 18 percent of the prison population.[23]

Although it is not our primary concern here, the link between crime and work and the labor movement has always been most important. Much police and other repressive state activity, including the growth of prisons, surrounded attempts to organize the labor force in the late nineteenth and early twentieth centuries.[24] It is also important to note the relationship between "organized crime" and business, and the very fine line separating the two.[25] In any event, the historical stage of capitalism and the social usefulness of a worker's labor are important determinants of the way in which he will take part in the struggle for survival.

In the corporate liberal state, repression occurs through the mechanisms of formal legal rationality. Forms of collective violence and rebellion are defined and treated as individual crimes. This is designed to convince participants and others that such violence is nothing more than ordinary "criminality," and to negate arguments, demands, and heightened political consciousness, which emerge from such struggles. Once participants in struggle have been given the status of "criminal," their claims have been deemed illegitimate, and they are unlikely to receive support from other groups in society. Those who may be sympathetic and/or those who are involved in the administration of "criminal justice" are concerned only with ensuring that the proper "rights" of these criminal suspects are being respected and that "due process" is followed, and not with substantive matters of who is being dealt with and why.[26] In this way, a political struggle is turned into a legal battle, and the revolutionary potential of the movement is minimized. In the process, the legitimacy of the entire formal legal apparatus and the political economic context within which it operates are reinforced.

If we are to understand the unrest, "rioting," and political movements in prisons today, we must begin to see that it is the prisons and capitalist society that perpetrate violence against the inmates and not vice versa. The prisons, as part of the repressive state apparatus,[27] function by violent means to ensure the domination of the ruling class over the working class. The role of the repressive state apparatus consists of securing by force (physical, administrative, and otherwise) and ideological control the political conditions under which the same social relations of production and power can be reproduced, and under which the production of ruling-class ideology can occur.

The ideologies of crime, rehabilitation, and parole reinforce the idea that some individuals just refuse to live peacefully among the rest of us and need to be punished, reformed, treated, corrected, or whatever the current rhetoric of the time is. Crime is seen in terms of aberrant, incorrectly socialized individuals who must be made to fit back into existing structures that had no use for them in the first place. Crime is not seen as a class phenomenon and its political meaning is mystified. Because crime and "criminals" are outside of the actual process of production and on the fringes of society, it is difficult to relate "common criminality" to a class struggle. However, most of those who commit crimes are in effect questioning the fundamental operation of society. Most prisoners are part of the reserve army of labor, people for whom, at various points in their life, there is no work or only work which leaves them on or below subsistence level. Although they may or may not have a subjective political consciousness or class analysis of how the larger social system impinges on and determines to a great extent the reality of their lives, in fact, objectively their behavior exists and can be understood only in terms of that particular class structure and the contradictions and deteriorating social relations of advanced capitalism.[28] "Criminals" are the "victims" of social conditions that are at the heart of political struggles, and are very much prisoners "politically,"[29] in terms of the structure of power within the United States. Imprisonment, as a form of punishment by the state, is an intrinsically political act. As David Gordon points out, nearly all crimes in capitalist societies represent perfectly *rational* responses to the structure of institutions upon which capitalist societies are based.[30]

A study summarizing experience with correctional programs concluded that:

It is difficult to escape the conclusion that the act of incarcerating a person at all will impair whatever potential he has for crime-free future adjustment, and that regardless of which "treatments" are administered while he is in prison, the longer he is kept there the more will he deteriorate and the more likely it is that he will recidivate.[31]

Based upon results such as these, it is difficult not to see imprisonment and parole in terms of elimination. However, the researchers who conducted the investigation quoted from above, and others like them, did not see this as anything other than accidental. They suggest that it is time to "call off the game," since "nothing much is won if either side wins."[32] It is as if we merely had to change our ideas or consciousness to create changes in prisons. These researchers do not see that one side has a tremendous amount at stake in the "game," and that there are objective material conditions that support the process of imprisonment as it is. Until those conditions are changed, prisons and parole will not change.

Parole and the Political Use of Social Science

To carry out the real task of imprisonment, the elimination of groups from the excess population that threaten the existing social order and the preservation of class interests the criminal justice system serves, both the ideology of "prediction" and the ideology of "seriousness" are maintained. The focus of most criminological research on parole has not been on the board, but on the inmates and prediction. This concept supports and justifies positivist notions of quantification and statistical measurement, the ideology of treatment, and the whole "medical model." However, the element of "offense severity" has not been ignored. Let us investigate these two concepts, "prediction" and "severity," along with the third concept that forms the basis of the new parole board guidelines, "amount of time to be served," to understand the specific practice of the board and, especially, the political nature of social science.

The federal parole statutes indicate that one of the grounds upon which parole is to be granted is whether there is a reasonable probability that a prisoner will live and remain at liberty without violating the law.[33] This would suggest selection based on the potential risk of recidivism. It is here that criminologists have focused the bulk of their research, and they have asked the administrative question, "is the Parole Board using the right factors for selection?" As a member of the National Institute of Law Enforcement and Criminal Justice pointed out,

... important benefits would ensue if we could find out what kinds of information in what amounts make a significant difference in the decisions of a Parole Board ... a standard could be established which would assure the collection of those information items which make a difference ... what kinds of information are we talking about? I think we have operationally defined the information we want as those items which can be statistically related to the chances of success or failure after release.[34]

Contained within the concept of prediction of success on parole is the issue of rehabilitation.[35] Although the board and many criminologists argued that elements indicating rehabilitation were most important in making the determination of who to parole and who to deny, our empirical study shows a contradiction. Predictors indicating these factors did not have an important effect on the parole decision. We have also seen from the previous investigation of the case of David Donner that rehabilitation and risk were not the consideration, nor were they the consideration in the three cases cited in Appendix 3A. The board has published formal and informal lists of criteria related to the issue of its decisions and the risk of potential recidivism, but these have not been used. The "criteria" serve as an effective ideological tool for mystification.

Many of the contradictions stem from the difference in the approach of the classical school of thought regarding crime, from which "corrections" personnel are coming, and positivist thought, from which researchers begin. The ideological position of board members has been that each individual case should be studied on its own merits in subjective fashion (based on the notion of free will of the individual), and the ideological argument of criminologists is that scientific, objective standardizing provides for greater effectiveness (based on ideas of social determinism). To compromise with its critics, the board issued statements of criteria, thus appearing to join the positivists in their regard for "science."[36] However, members continued to believe and support the principle that each individual "criminal" should be considered separately as unique.[37] Board members have consistently pointed out that experience or prediction tables will not take the place of "clinical" judgment, compassion, or concern for a particular individual.[38] Members indicate that statistical tables will not take the job of decision making away from board members, but will merely be a supplement to their "skill and experience." The use of words such as "clinical" case study and individualized "diagnosis" and treatment, in typical jargon borrowed from psychology, is an attempt to grant status and legitimacy to the whole process of arguing that the skill and experience of an individual board member are superior to statistical methods. There is also a serious contradiction here for positivist criminologists. On the one hand, they spend their energies creating experience tables and base expectancy scores for predicting success on parole. They are well aware that board members have not used experience tables in the past and shy away from using them now.[39] Researchers have even supported and legitimated the board's disregard of prediction tables in favor of its own arbitrary and subjective conceptualizations.[40] However, they have done this by saying it is necessary to go "beyond prediction" to "greater complexity," rather than agreeing outright that the board's subjective interpretations are valid. It is becoming obvious that the whole rhetoric surrounding "prediction" must come under more detailed scrutiny.

Some sociologists have criticized techniques used in predictive studies because of the absence of an adequate theoretical framework that would give significance to the statistical manipulations.[41] These people have been critical of the fact that parole has been studied largely from the narrow focus of predicting success or failure, or conceived of primarily as a source of data on the outcome of "treatment."[42] Predictive studies have also been attacked by liberal critics because many qualitative elements surrounding "success" on parole have been ignored. Such studies have looked primarily at what are presumed to be static features of a particular individual. Recidivism has been regarded simply as the function of a parolee's characteristics or behavior, and any activities of the parole agent or supervisory organization have been neglected. These critics suggest that study is needed of the entire parole network as a complex organization, and that parole success is not a result of background characteristics, but of factors such as case loads of parole officers, parole agent discretion, and parolee-agent interaction. They point to studies that demonstrate that when parole supervision increases, more illegal behavior "occurs" (is found).[43]

Another problem with prediction is the fact that it does not necessarily work for individuals. When deciding whether to keep a person confined on the basis of a prediction of his supposed dangerousness, many individuals are mistakenly predicted to be dangerous.[44] In fact, the incidence of "false positives" is very high, whether one uses statistical or case-study devices.[45] Also, any system of preventive incarceration conceals the number of persons confined erroneously, but reveals those released erroneously. Once decision makers see that some of those released do commit new crimes, they seek to expand the number of those who are confined to reduce incorrect decisions. In doing this, they are necessarily increasing the number of those confined erroneously. They must do this to protect their own careers from public critics who would hold them responsible.

Another element that must be considered in discussing prediction is the fact that we cannot predict a specific act of violence will occur because there are so many dialectical elements within any interactional situation, for which there are no adequate controls. Violence and "criminal" tendencies are not fixed inherent qualities of individuals[46] but, rather, are dependent upon circumstances and material structures and are not a matter of simple free will and individual, subjective consciousness. Many researchers like to separate "violent" from "property" or "victimless" crimes. However, the commission of "violent" crime is for the most part related to lack of certain basic needs not provided by society and the frustrations produced by social life. Crimes of violence are infrequent events. They are difficult to predict both because they are rare and because they are situational. Crimes of "property" and related crimes of "violence" can be generally predicted to continue to be committed in a society where so many have-nots are created who have a difficult time maintaining their existence, while the few who have property continue to increase their stronghold. Such crimes can best be considered as strategies for survival.

It is the contention here, then, that the attention focused on the element of prediction provides a smokescreen that helps to mystify the real parole-selection process. We are led to believe that if we could predict success accurately, if our statistical techniques and data-collection methods were improved, the parole procedure and imprisonment itself would be more "effective." If prediction of success on parole was the major interest of the board, then those committed for sexual crimes and crimes of force against persons would be released earlier because those convicted of these kinds of crimes generally do not repeat them.

Offenses against the person, compared with property offenses, are more often found in the favorable parole outcome group.[47]

For example, the board regarded the commission of a sexual offense as counting against release, while the success rate for sexual offenders was higher than that for most other categories of offense.[48]

Earlier release for such people is not the case. Also, many inmates would be released at the time of first hearing, which is also not the case. "Those who were paroled at the first hearing were more often found in the favorable parole performance category."[49] More people are denied parole or continued for further review than released on parole at their first hearing. Thus, there are factors other than rehabilitation, prediction, and success on parole that the board considers important.

We can illustrate this point with the following comment by a criminologist involved in a study of parole decision making:

A homicide case appears before the board with a high prediction of success—let's say a prediction based on experience that shows that 85 percent of the people appearing before you with such characteristics will succeed on parole. He hasn't done much time, the offense was rough and there is no convincing plan for his employment or residence after release. I am sure that you deny him, despite the favorable prediction; the fifteen percent likelihood of failure is too much to accept. But you might well accept that fifteen percent if you were considering the case of a chronic petty thief who had always limited himself to thievery. Indeed, you probably would accept an even higher likelihood of failure. In effect, you would be taking into account the significance of information items which the computer could not and, I think, never will be able to allow for.[50]

What are the "information items which the computer could not and never will be able to allow for?" These are undoubtedly the specific value judgments made by board members and other powerful agents as to what constitutes serious crime for which individuals need to be punished, and what amounts of time inmates must serve to have received that "just" punishment. Computers do not take into account the task of elimination of specific troublesome groups of people, although they could probably be programmed to do so if this task of imprisonment became openly known and supported politically. At present, however, the ideology has been rehabilitation, not punishment, and therefore the element of seriousness is supposed to be secondary to treatment. If at all possible, the board prefers to use potential of unsuccessful parole as its reason to deny, rather than seriousness of offense, which would be a contradiction to the rhetoric of rehabilitation. The board falls back on seriousness, however, much of the time, for individuals appear too readily to be "rehabilitated."[51]

The other statutory element upon which the board relies is a general catch-all statement that parole may be granted if such release is not incompatible with the welfare of society. This involves a value judgment about protecting some abstract entity called "society," and has in effect been translated by the board as relating to punishment and deterrence.[52] Individuals who, according to prediction devices, are good parole risks, are often kept in prison longer because of the board's judgment regarding the seriousness of their offense.

A study of parole criteria by a law professor pointed out that the probability of recidivism is by no means the sole concern of a parole board.[53] Parole boards often deny parole for other reasons, such as (1) the need to enforce prison discipline and therefore deny parole for poor institutional adjustment, (2) the obligation to protect the public from those who have shown themselves capable of assaultive behavior (of "serious" crimes), (3) the fact that an inmate might have served too little time for the institution to really "get to know him" and his case,[54] (4) so the inmate can benefit from prison programs,[55] and (5) to avoid criticism of the parole system should the inmate commit a new crime.

It would appear that the rubric of "seriousness" could apply to every crime for which individuals appear for a parole hearing. First, the board does not deal with anyone who received less than a 180-day (six-month) sentence, for no one with a sentence less than six months is eligible for parole. Right from the beginning, those whose crimes were considered by the court to be less "serious," and/or those who were considered by the court to be "good risks" have already been sifted out. Second, those whose crimes are categorized by the board as having low or low to moderate severity generally receive short sentences and serve them out. As the board itself points out:

In contrast to bank robbers, those convicted of immigration law violations receive parole only a small percent of the time. This is generally so because of the short sentence they receive. . . . Drug law offenders tend to receive parole rather frequently because of their long sentences. . . . Selective Service law violators who receive long sentences generally often receive parole, while those who are given short sentences are not paroled.[56]

The empirical study presented earlier indicates that very small percentages of those convicted of "low" and "low to moderate" severity offenses were paroled.[57] All of this means that everyone else the board considers can be said to have committed a "serious" crime and can be set off and continued for a rehearing or denied parole based upon this factor.[58]

Criminologists have been aware that severity of offense is an issue in the paroling process. However, research funding for studies in this area has obviously not been as lucrative as for studies of prediction. What has been done is to test whether a consensus exists among various groups about what seriousness is. Again positivist social science has begun with the assumption that there is a basic agreement within society about the essence and universality of "seriousness," which can be discovered and measured through use of quantitative and "scientific" methods. Researchers have set about trying to learn what that consensus is. There is no consideration of the possibility that parole boards or any other powerful group of persons related to or influencing them have made the determination about what constitutes a "serious" crime and what this order of seriousness is.

For example, T. Sellin and M. Wolfgang point out, in their "pioneering" and well-known work, *The Measurement of Delinquency*,[59] that the "criteria for determining degrees of seriousness of crimes must ultimately be determined by someone's or some group's subjective interpretation," and that "no external objective criteria, beyond people's judgments, exists for producing a continuum of seriousness of delinquent acts."[60] However, they decided that this problem could be overcome if judgments were elicited from "theoretically meaningful and large social groups" whose consensus would produce a series of weighted values that would have validity. Sellin and Wolfgang felt there were objective methods of measurement that had been developed into psychological "laws" and that these methods could be applied to measures of seriousness. They spent several pages of their book equating this process with the way in which the physical sciences deal with transformations from qualitative to quantitative variables.[61] Sellin and Wolfgang believed that legal definitions and sanctions came from the "middle-class value system"; therefore, they selected university students, police officers, and juvenile court judges as groups that would be representative of this normative structure.[62] If there is any agreement between these groups (and there are many reasons why we can expect some, since they come from similar ethnic and class backgrounds with similarly socialized attitudes, life-styles, adaptations, aspirations, perceptions, and are primarily white males), it cannot be accepted without looking at the ideological hegemony exercised by the dominant ruling class, which has the power to maintain its definitions and world view.[63] Sellin and Wolfgang, however, did not do this, and were delighted to find that, indeed, there was a consensus between these three groups.

Several other studies in Canada and Puerto Rico sought to replicate and support Sellin and Wolfgang's work, and did find agreement among students, judges, police, white-collar workers, and even lower class juveniles.[64]

Taking their cue from Sellin and Wolfgang's example, P. Rossi et al.[65] sought to confirm, in the face of the new force of "conflict" theory[66] which implies disagreement over what is to be considered "serious," that there is indeed a consensus. A list of 140 offenses was presented in 200 interviews with a sample of the adult black and white population of Baltimore, chosen from census tract data. This was thought to be a more representative population than Sellin and Wolfgang's. As anticipated, the general ordering of crimes accorded with "common-sense" expectations. Crimes against persons were rated more serious than crimes against property and disturbing the peace. Crimes against persons known to the offender were regarded as less serious than those committed against strangers. White-collar crime (as represented by embezzlement and price gouging) and "crimes without victims" (such as homosexuality) were not regarded as particularly serious.[67] Blacks and women tended to rate each crime as more serious than whites and males. There was a high correlation between blacks and whites, men and women, and less and better educated persons. However, "poorly educated" black males disagreed most with other subgroups in the sample. The authors do not investigate why this is so, other than to imply that the lack of education on the part of black males accounts for this disagreement. Again it is seen as a problem of inadequate and incorrect socialization. The authors discuss the concept of a "subculture of violence," which exists among lower class groups, that defines certain acts differently. This is why a crime such as "beating up an acquaintance" is regarded less seriously among "poorly educated" blacks. The act is not seen as an adaptation or reaction to conditions within the class structure, but in terms of a put-down, "The line between manly sport and crime can be thin indeed."[68]

In sum, these researchers, too, determine that the extent of consensus among subgroups is impressive. What they do not realize is that they have measured the extensive ideological hegemony exercised by the powerful in maintaining definitions of crime and a scale of seriousness of crime beneficial to them.

The National Council on Crime and Delinquency, in its 1970-72 parole decision-making project, recognized that the concept of "offense severity" was important in the parole board's determination. Part of their study was therefore designed to "develop procedures for more consistent offense-severity judgments."[69] Here is another example of researchers supplying technique rather than critique, for the problem was narrowly conceptualized in terms of providing for consistency between board members, rather than focusing on the issue of measuring "severity" in the first place. The researchers devised tests for agreement between the eight hearing examiners and eight board members. Categories developed from these small experiments were incorporated into the new parole board guidelines for decision-making. Merely because 16 board members and hearing examiners can come to some agreement regarding definitions of serious crimes does not mean their conceptualizations are essential truths. Hearing examiners and board members are politically selected, and if detailed examination of their backgrounds was made, many similarities would probably be found. Persons whose world view was different would not be selected to be on the board. One board member who disagreed was not reappointed.[70]

The third element of the new guidelines that must be considered is "amount of time to be served" or "severity of punishment." This appears to be an arbitrary designation, unrelated to later success or recidivism. The inmates could just as easily have served 20 minutes as 20 months. Studies have shown that there is no relationship between time served and probability of recidivism, other than the fact that keeping people in prison longer increases that probability.[71] However, the empirical study presented earlier indicated that "time served" and "length of sentence" were the most valuable predictors for parole decision outcome. This means that although the board claims to consider each case on its individual merits, there is in fact a general pattern or policy as far as time in prison is concerned. The board itself points out that it has been equalizing sentences:

It is clear that the multiplicity of sentencing choices available to the courts, and the varying attitudes between sentencing judges results in a wide disparity in the lengths of sentences imposed for persons convicted of similar offenses, and often who possess similar backgrounds. To a very real degree, the Board of Parole tends, in practice, to equalize this disparity whenever it is not bound to the one-third minimum time required in "regular" sentences.[72]

The board has also reported that:

Selective service law violators who receive long sentences generally often receive parole, while those who are given short sentences are not paroled. Thus, for this type of offender, a relative balance between individuals and time served is thus achieved by the Board despite the wide disparity in sentencing practices by the courts.

and

The figures in . . . illustrate a remarkable similarity in time served prior to parole regardless of the type of sentencing procedure used by the courts. Adults with definite sentences serve approximately the same period of time as those with indeterminate sentences.[73]

In Chapter 3, it was pointed out that predictors indicating potential for success on parole did not have an important effect on the parole decision. The amount of time served did.[74] The time to be served on the new parole board guidelines was not determined by the potential or prediction of success on parole. It was, rather, related to the factor "severity of offense." We can see this in the following discussion by the research staff of the National Council on Crime and Delinquency (NCCD), which developed the guidelines for the board.

For each of a set of offense ratings (offense behavior descriptions) coded by the project, the median time served was calculated. Offense ratings with similar median times served were combined to produce six severity level classifications.[75]

Offense and offense severity thus appear to be the major determinants of amount of time to be served. The researchers who developed the guidelines took as unalterable givens the times served for the offenses described. Then they "produced" six levels of severity classification. This is an extremely subjective process, which they attempt to present as objective in their report.[76] The earlier empirical study indicates, however, that there is a contradiction regarding time served. It appeared there that the ranges of time to be served indicated on the guidelines did not come from actual past practice by the board. A great percentage of persons who had served time within or greater than the ranges on the guidelines were not paroled. It is not known why the times served in the sample do not match the median times served determined by the NCCD. Perhaps it has something to do with the "smoothing . . . performed to increase the consistency of these medians," and the fact that "the size of the appropriate range was determined after informal discussions with several board members and hearing examiners and, while arbitrary, is to some extent proportional to the size of the median."[77] The guidelines make explicit the implicit policy of determining times to be served before parole based on the offense committed and a subjective judgment of "severity." The element of parole prognosis is simply thrown in to satisfy potential liberal critics and positivist social scientists who have developed elaborate predictive devices and who retain some remnants from the notion of rehabilitation. The creation of the guidelines legitimates and increases the board's control over the making of parole decisions in the way in which it wishes. Since board decisions could be predicted by knowledge of what the board considered regarding offense severity and parole prognosis, the NCCD incorporated these as "objective measures" into the new guidelines, indicating that it was developing an explicit indicant of parole-selection policy.[78] It was doing no more than supplying a technical service to a political administrative body. Is this what social science is all about?

If prediction is not the only, or even the overriding, consideration of parole boards, then neither is rehabilitation, for rehabilitation is contained within the rubric of "prediction." If "seriousness" is the most important consideration, then retribution (punishment and deterrence) becomes the reason for imprisonment. Normal Carlson, federal director of prisons, recently pointed out:

For the last few years in particular, most people in this field . . . have assumed that rehabilitation is the only rationale for incarceration, that people are sentenced primarily for that purpose. But . . . federal and state prison officials who made this assumption are beginning to reevaluate the role of prisons in society and are concluding that imprisonment chiefly is a means of punishment and deterrence.[79]

A recent article in the *Los Angeles Times* pointed out openly that in California changes in policy have put retribution before rehabilitation. The three key elements in California's new parole policy are that: (1) punishment should fit the crime; (2) inmates should know how much time they can expect to spend behind bars; and (3) rehabilitation, although still attempted, should not be a condition of parole. The new parole policy was initiated at a time when there was pending legislation to abolish the 58-year old law instituting the indeterminate sentence and to sharply curtail the power of the Adult Authority (California's parole board). Raymond Procunier, Governor Brown's appointee as chairman of the California Adult Authority, pointed out:

It's cruel and unusual punishment for a man not to know how much time he's going to do. Board members used to deny parole dates for the wrong reasons. They would search for some reason to deny a man when the real reason he was denied was he didn't have enough time served for his crime. I don't think it's possible to expect a person to get better in prison. I think they ought to be sent there for punishment. I think people can really relate to honest punishment.[80]

Procunier predicted that removing the uncertainty from inmate's lives would significantly reduce prison unrest and violence. The Adult Authority developed guidelines similar to the U.S. Board of Parole's, which specified time ranges to be served for particular crimes. Thus, an inmate no longer has to participate in prison "programs," but can sit in his cell the whole time and be released as long as he conforms to institutional rules. This is all being done in the name of humanitarian concern for people in prison.

Procunier claimed this is a radical departure from previous policy. Some disagree, for as he himself admits, parole board practice has always been to base decisions on the offense committed and a subjective determination of sufficient time served. It is a change in the official ideological rhetoric surrounding the practice of parole, to stop pretending that rehabilitation is a consideration and openly declare that retribution is what prisons are there for. We are back where we started. What is important is that many of the myths surrounding "individualized treatment," the "medical model" of criminality, and "rehabilitation within prison," are swept away and more of the reality of prison is exposed. From here, an analysis of prisons from the larger perspective of political power, class structure and economic relationships can more readily be made.

C. Wright Mills pointed out that academic discussion of social problems that does not proceed in terms of the struggle for power within a society is interesting only in the political uses made of it by those in power.[81] The previous examples of research are indicative of how inquiry in the social sciences has been operating in the service of powerful elements in society. We must begin to analyze this problem.

The similarity between military activity abroad and crime control at home is becoming clearer. The recent war in Vietnam was part of the same war being waged domestically against oppressed groups within the United States. For example, advisors to the President's Crime Commission noted that:

The experience of science in the military, however, suggests that a fruitful collaboration can be established between criminal justice officials on one hand and engineers, physicists, economists, and social behavioral scientists on the other. In military research organizations these different professions, working with military officers in interdisciplinary teams, have attacked defense problems in new ways and have provided insights that were new even to those with long military experience. Similar developments appear possible in criminal justice.[82]

Thus, the use of science and technology to increasingly rationalize "crime control" is being legitimated and encouraged, much as this has occurred for military purposes.[83] Criminology is an important part of that social science they are talking about. Criminologists have become part of the process by which the capitalist system maintains its hegemony, by supplying the latest theoretical and technical knowledge and technicians and personnel to operate inside administrative machines, and by producing ideological arguments that support and legitimate the practice of control.

The direction of most research in the social sciences is determined by the amount and source of funding for such endeavors. Control of these resources is in the hands of forces outside the universities, the large foundations, and the government agencies that finance and help to create intellectual doctrines. Many years ago, C. Wright Mills pointed out the still valid observation:

Research in social science is increasingly dependent upon funds from foundations, and foundations are notably averse to scholars who develop unpopular theses, that is, those placed in the category of "unconstructive." The United States' growing international entanglements have subtle effects upon some American intellectuals: to the young man who teaches and writes on Latin America, Asia, or Europe and who refrains from deviating from acceptable facts and policies, these entanglements lead to a voluntary censorship. He hopes for opportunities of research, travel, and foundation subsidies. The means of effective communication are being expropriated from the intellectual worker. The material basis of his initiative and intellectual freedom is no longer in his hands. Some intellectuals feel these processes in their work. They know more than they say and they are powerless and afraid.[84]

The trend in academia towards professors as "hired heads" of the powerful corporate class is not a matter of individual professors and intellectuals "selling out." There are structural reasons why this occurs. Professors are interested in building careers, and these center on available job opportunities, which are within increasingly bureaucratized institutions. Most importantly, the professional ideology of "value-free science" is one where political involvement is seen as "unscientific" and antithetical to the "discovery" of truth. A professor may become a political tool without being aware that this has happened, for he sees himself as apolitical and justly so.

Let us examine one example of the subservience of criminology to power. It is interesting to look at the study of parole decision making by the National Council on Crime and Delinquency, whose data were used in doing the empirical investigation in Chapter 3, and analyze their research in terms similar to those used by Mills in his discussion of sociological studies of industrial relations.[85] An analogy can be made between research in industrial relations and research in criminology.

We have no difficulty answering the question posed by Howard Becker in his article, "Whose Side Are We On?"[86] It is obvious from the beginning that the research staff involved in the NCCD study of parole is on the side of the powerful, in this case the federal parole board and funding agencies supporting the research. The NCCD wished to "provide assistance to decision-makers."[87]

The general aim of the project was to develop, test, and demonstrate programs of improved information for decision-making by providing objective, relevant information for individual case decisions, and by summarizing experience with parole as an aid to improved policy decisions . . . and to aid paroling authorities in rational decision-making for increased effectiveness of prison release procedures.[88]

The problem was conceived of as, "Given the present state of knowledge, what is the best thing to do [decide] about this individual, now . . . what is a rational decision under conditions of uncertainty. Developments in scientific thought, specifically as a by-product of the application of science in wartime through 'operations research,' have led to some convergence between the decision-makers and the research scientists."[89] The NCCD study was done in collaboration with the U.S. Board of Parole, the Federal Bureau of Investigation, Administrative Office of the United States Courts, Federal Bureau of Prisons, most adult parole systems in the United States, National Advisory Committee of the National Probation and Parole Institutes, and the National Institute of Law Enforcement and Criminal Justice of the Law Enforcement Assistance Administration. We are not given an indication of the power each group wielded. The summary report praises the cooperation and assistance of these agencies for supplying needed information and services promptly and efficiently. It is not surprising that they secured such cooperation, considering that all involved were perceiving the task and the problem in the same way, and that support and legitimation, rather than questioning and criticism, were the main goals of the researchers.

Throughout the fourteen reports of their study, the NCCD serves as spokesman and apologist for the U.S. Board of Parole. There is no comment or critique of board positions, but rather, these positions are merely stated. For example,

It is the opinion of the Board that release under some form of official supervision and control is more likely to achieve success than outright release without such supervision and control.

and

Other goals rated as important by federal parole board members were the encouragement of inmate program participation and the release of persons on the basis of individual response and progress within the prison.[90]

The NCCD reports are filled with unclear, ambiguous, and obscure verbage, so we are not always sure what is being said. For example, in discussing the fact that measurement of risk is not the only concern in parole decision making, they point out that

Only the quite unsophisticated would argue, however, that the measurement of parole risk in these terms is the only (or even the overriding) issue in parole decision-making. Other concerns relate to sanctioning, to due process, to system-regulatory, and to citizen representation objectives.[91]

The issue is then dropped, with brief mention of the fact that more attention to decision objectives is needed. The elements of supposed concern are not discussed. We do not even know what these terms mean here. Although the researchers suggest that predictive devices are not as important as has been thought, they express confidence that "improvement in prediction" can be made. They suggest a form of prediction called "individual prediction," which might be possible if and when different kinds of data become available.

In doing some "self-criticism," there is a brief discussion of problems of doing research.

A distinction is noted between research aimed at the production of instruments for operational use and research investigations. It seems that fundamental research cannot be divorced from operational research, and vice versa. There are now noted problems arising out of operational research requiring a kind of research approach which would normally be considered as "fundamental research," before more progress is probable. One important area is that of investigation of the processes of decision-making. The information search strategies of decision-makers (as well as the goals they seek) are important but little understood at the present time. There is clearly a relationship between "degrees of belief" and "probability," and there are very important issues of moral values which impinge upon research methods. It is thought that the present methods whereby research funds become available may not be such that an optimal research strategy is to be developed. It is considered that the relevance of research to social problems is not related to whether the research is at a high or low level of abstraction. High levels of abstraction may also be highly relevant; the difficulty arises in demonstrating this.[92]

We see here, in rather confusing and undeveloped language, a statement of the problem of obtaining research funds to investigate relevant issues. But a clear explanation of problems that arose during this study is not given. They seem to be indicating that a theoretical basis has been missing from their study, which was designed to produce an administrative instrument. We have to guess at the meaning of such terms as "degrees of belief" and "probability." We are given no examples of high and low levels of abstraction. What is being said is not coming through, and we would imagine there are political reasons behind this vague and ambiguous dialogue.

C. Wright Mills analyzed the field of industrial sociology from the critical perspective of political economy. In discussing the shift of emphasis in sociology towards changing business needs, Mills pointed out how social science produced the legitimation for new powerful groups of what he called "sophisticated conservatives." The greater scale and complexity of business and the concentration of power, along with competition from unions and the enlargement of the state apparatus, caused a shift in emphasis from laissez-faire to liberal policies. Ideologically, this resulted in studies of "human relations in industry." Although cloaked in terms of developing the full potential of employees, creating mutual understanding, and enlarging democratic tradition, these studies were, in effect, attempts to help management devise ways of organizing the work process so workers could produce more goods in less time and thus lower production costs, keep disgruntled workers happy and ease tensions, and find new ways of justifying the concentrated power exercised in the economic and social realms.[93] Mills went on to examine the latent assumptions upon which sociological studies of "industrial relations" rested, to isolate key themes and the moral and political perspectives thus revealed. These themes can also be found in the NCCD study of parole.

1. The perspective taken is that of the managerial administrative elite. The work undertaken by the researchers is to serve these people. This has determined the structure of the research, conceptualization of problems, explanatory models, and conclusions. The purpose is technical, stated from the managerial viewpoint and translatable into managerial tasks, rather than in terms of human beings in power relationships. The whole organizational edifice is assumed as unalterably given. The issue is how to further the progress of the group and the success of its operations. Criminology here has retreated from political and economic conflicts to the administration of managerial functions.

2. The problem is seen as one of acquiring the cooperation and collaboration of everyone involved in the enterprise, including the inmates, while quelling the protest of critics. Time is spent showing how "fairness" and "justice" are being dealt with.[94] The impression is that now critics and inmates themselves should have no cause for grievance and should accept the legitimacy of the board because it is going to be "fair" and "equitable" in standardizing time to be served. The aim is to minimize threats and potential disruption through objectification and routinization of policy. However, the discussion of "fairness" and "justice" proceeds in an ahistorical vacuum, isolated from larger political issues of power and powerlessness. It is somewhat like an abstract Socratic puzzle.

The concept of fairness is not exactly the same as the concept of justice. There is, however, seldom any clear distinction made in the use of the two terms in law. Some dictionaries define "fairness" as lack of injustice, but the absence of injustice is not the same as the presence of justice—thus "justice" is not defined as fairness but rather as "an accord with truth." That is to say, there seems to be reasonable agreement among authorities of English usage that nothing can be just which is unfair; but fairness is not necessarily justice; or justice includes fairness but is more demanding. It may be that we could claim that this is because fairness is a relative term, but justice implies absolute values. . . . Ensuring justice (accord with truth/law) also ensures fairness. In the first case (justice) there is an external criterion. In the second case (fairness) the elements can be in adjustment with each other but are not necessarily in accord with respect to an external criterion. By "fairness" we mean that *similar* persons are dealt with in *similar* ways in *similar* situations. . . . Will an individual, then, see his treatment as "fair" if he seems himself as (in all significant ways) similar to another person who received exactly similar treatment? Not quite, since it would seem to require more than one other person—it would not be unreasonable to claim that both were treated unfairly. However, as the sample of "similar" persons increases, so the idea of similar treatments among that sample becomes more likely to be regarded as "fair."[95]

This metaphysical argument relates "fairness" to statistical concepts of similarity and sample size, rather than to specific historical situations of power and powerlessness.

3. In the NCCD study, no mention is made that the crimes for which people are imprisoned and then considered for parole are almost invariably those committed by the lower class poor. The list of offenses for which individuals are paroled, as indicated on the board's guidelines, does not include crimes committed by corporations (which are generally treated through the civil courts or administratively), political crimes (such as Watergate and the crimes of the FBI and CIA), and any number of crimes essentially more damaging to the structure of society than lower class, minority, and small, everyday, individual street crimes. The crimes perpetrated by the elite are not punished by the elite. There is further evidence of class bias in the guidelines, for the elements that make up the "salient-factor score" discriminate against blacks, minorities, and the poor who do not have these qualities in their backgrounds in the first place.

4. There is a total absence in the NCCD study of the element of power. The researchers do not focus on the power holders or the law or the social construction of "crimes," but take these as given and focus on "offenders" as they have been defined. Bland, neutral, and meaningless terms are used throughout the reports to obscure relations of power. Such terms as "effectiveness," "improvement," "structuring discretion," "consistency," "making implicit policy explicit," and "rationality and appropriateness of policy" are not defined in terms of the social structure and material conditions of political and economic reality. Parole selection is compared to the insurance business and selection for risk there.[96] However, in the process of parole, unlike insurance, the element of risk is not a good predictor of decision outcome. Time served according to severity of offense and length of sentence is the best predictor. Decisions to parole are not made based upon prediction, and it therefore cannot be compared to insurance to neutralize and mystify the process.

5. The way in which prisons and parole boards attempt to manipulate the prisoners is not recognized in the NCCD study, since the dimension of power is overlooked. The only manipulation that occurs is that of "data." Even this is a problem because the data is of such poor quality that sophisticated statistical techniques cannot be applied.[97] The researchers see here an analogy to the physical sciences, which further legitimates what they are doing as "scientific:"

High quality ore is needed if powerful methods of extraction are to be used; poor quality ore can be used in rougher methods of extraction.[98]

Although the researchers point out the fundamental problem of the quality of the raw material in criminal justice decision making, this is the data they have used in creating the decision guidelines, and they do not suggest what should be done to "develop better quality data."

6. The NCCD assumed a consensus model of social order.[99] The aims and desires of the "people" were seen as synonymous with those of the parole board. Even inmates were seen to want the same order:

This procedure should substantially reduce the present uncertainty felt by inmates under indeterminate sentences as to when they will actually be released (and as to what they must accomplish to obtain this release).[100]

The idea of the board serving the public interest, as well as that of inmates, is perpetuated. The board is presented as protector of the general welfare and stability of the system through skilled and enlightened selection of parolees.

7. The latent political formula hidden within such research is that of preserving the status quo, which is the system of capitalism. The aim is to smooth and continue the parole board practice of exercising discretion by effecting certain inexpensive reforms that do not measurably alter the process. In developing guidelines for the Board of Parole, the NCCD research staff placed itself in direct service to a political body engaged in the task of controlling prisoners. Supplying statistical technique and ideological legitimacy for the board's policy and procedures, the NCCD is an example of a criminology that provides the modern state with the most advanced system of control for the maintenance of domestic order, much as science and technology are being used for military purposes abroad.

The U.S. Board of Parole has been besieged by critics from the press, Congress, groups such as the American Civil Liberties Union, and the legal profession. There have been no critical studies from the field of sociology or criminology. Instead, the administrative problems of parole boards have been seen as problems for criminologists. David Horowitz[101] has pointed out in a similar vein that there have been no independent academic studies of so large and influential a corporation as Standard Oil. Journalists are more enlightened about its operations than sociologists. Horowitz indicates that this is an example of how totally academic social science has overlooked the matrices of power and interest that are determinant forces of policy and development. We must recognize the political nature of science. No scientist is independent of the social and economic system, which provides funds for research along with the kinds of questions to be asked and the uses to which research will be put. Much of social "science" is in fact ideological. This layer of ideology must be scraped away before we can begin to see the real social relations that lie beneath it. The ideology of parole is part of the ideological fortress that mystifies the experience and practice of control and imprisonment. If we begin to demystify this practice, we can hopefully begin to change it.

If there is one major insight gained from the foregoing analysis, it is that we are entering a transitional period in "corrections and penology." We are about to witness the end of the "medical model" and its attendant myths of "treatment and rehabilitation." Prisoners are no longer "sick." Instead, it appears that an attempt is being made to return ideologically to classical notions of criminals as "bad," morally inferior people who choose to neglect their social responsibilities and infringe on the "rights" of law-abiding citizens. Imprisonment is therefore once again simply punishment. However, the specific historical context in which such classical notions could flourish has now changed. It is no longer so ideologically believable in the context of corporate America as it was under competitive capitalism. The conditions and ideas that led to attempts at rehabilitation and treatment within prisons still remain. In order for the state and its formal legal machinery to continue to implement the policy of imprisonment, more repression by force rather than ideology will be necessary. For example, the indeterminate sentence was a primary means of maintaining prisons as functioning entities. The work of inmates has kept them going.[102] Inmates were induced to work because the carrot of parole was held up before them. In California, an inmate doing 2 to 10 or 5 to life (most sentences fall within these ranges) was at the total mercy of the parole board. He or she had to try to perform in the institution as well as possible to do less time. However, once the indeterminate sentence is gone and inmates know how much time they will have to do, the incentive to work in jobs that pay 4¢ to 24¢ per hour, if they pay at all, is also gone. Prisons will probably not be able to increase wages enough to make it interesting for inmates to do the primarily dead-end, uninteresting jobs that are available—laundry, cooking, cleaning, sewing, ironing, for example. It will be interesting to see what techniques are invented to make inmates work and keep prison institutions operating.[103] The labor of inmates not only serves to maintain the prisons as functioning entities, but also makes money for their keepers. Mitford compiled statistics that indicate how much profit prisons make off the labor of inmates.[104] For example, a prison dairy worker, whose production is valued at $14,279.00 and who gets an average wage of $3.40 a week, is worth 86 times his wage. In fact, Federal Prison Industries is the most profitable line of business in the country. Profits on sales in 1970 were 17 percent, and the average for all United States industries is 4.5 percent. From 1935 to 1970 the industries grossed $896 million.[105] War years are especially good to prison industries, since the army is a major customer. What is produced by convict labor is purchased by other governmental agencies, at a price equivalent to the retail market price. Prison Industries is very similar to the now outlawed convict contract-labor system, but instead of the inmate being farmed out, the work is farmed in. Convicts are still exploited as slave workers of the state. Mitford also points out that this systematic exploitation extends to the profits made by the state from interest on inmate trust accounts and illegal use of the Inmate Welfare Fund, profits made in prison canteens where goods are sold at much higher prices than outside, profits made from the sale of handicrafts made by the inmates, and profits made from the work furlough program.[106]

In any event, it seems that instead of reducing violence in prisons because prisoners will know how much time they have to serve, as suggested earlier by Procunier (as if this caused their violent behavior), getting rid of the indeterminate sentence may increase it. There will be less to threaten them with, other than boredom. Prisoners will have more time to cause "trouble," to get together politically and think and talk about what is going on. With the myth of rehabilitation and treatment gone, there will be a greater potential for anger on the part of inmates who see no hopes of better education, skills, or jobs, and this anger may be directed at the larger social structure that has put them in prison rather than inward towards themselves or each other. The contradictions between their situation in prison and that of corporate and political "criminals" outside may also become more apparent.

As George Jackson so eloquently put it:

... there are only two types of blacks ever released from these places. ... This camp brings out the very best in brothers or destroys them entirely. But none are unaffected. None who leave are normal. ... The broken men are so damaged that they will never again be suitable members of any sort of social unit. Everything that was still good when they entered the joint, anything inside of them that may have escaped the ruinous effects of black colonial existence, anything that may have been redeemable when they first entered the joint—is gone when they leave. ... [But], if I leave here alive, I'll leave nothing behind. ... I've been hungry too long. I've gotten angry too often. I've been lied to and insulted too many times. They've pushed me over the line from which there can be no retreat. I know that they will not be satisfied until they've pushed me out of this existence altogether. I've been the victim of so many racist attacks that I could never relax again. My reflexes will never be normal. I'm like a dog that has gone through the K-9 process. ... Up until now, the prospect of parole has kept us from confronting our captors with any real determination. But now, with the living conditions deteriorating, and with the sure knowledge that we are slated for destruction, we have been transformed into an implacable army of liberation.[107]

5 Summary and Conclusions: The Fate of Parole

Gather ye rose-buds while ye may,
Old Time is still a-flying;
And this same flower that smiles today,
Tomorrow will be dying.

Robert Herrick

The ideology and practice of parole is more complex than has been recognized. Some of the issues raised here in the context of parole include the entire question of the indeterminate sentence, the problem of rehabilitation and treatment, and the process of selecting inmates for release based on the elements of predicting risk of recidivism in individual cases, seriousness of crime, and time served. All of these issues bear a dialectical interrelationship to each other.

The concept of rehabilitation in a prison setting has recently been abandoned.[1] Prisons throughout the country are beginning to operate on the theory that the primary objective of imprisonment is the isolation and punishment of the "offender." Liberals and conservatives are embroiled in a controversy over this change of policy, which surprisingly puts some radicals and conservatives on the same side.

California is a good example of the form this controversy is taking. In 1975 the California Adult Authority (parole board) issued guidelines for decision-making similar to those of the U.S. Board of Parole. However, state courts ruled that such guidelines for fixed terms violated the law; that is, they violated the indeterminate sentence that required authorities to consider not only the inmate's crime, but his conduct in prison, his efforts toward rehabilitation, and his potential for safe release. The state supreme court indicated that the guidelines substituted a mechanized tit-for-tat in place of discriminating individual judgment.[2] Only the legislature should change the law. So the legislature did. On August 31, 1976 the state legislature passed Senate Bill 42, authored by Senator John Nejedly.[3] Governor Brown signed the bill into law in September, 1976. Under the bill, the indeterminate sentence becomes a thing of the past for 95 percent of those sent to California prisons.

Conservatives strongly supported the bill as a way of obtaining greater control over the process of law enforcement and punishment. Corrections personnel, middle-level agents who had to bear the brunt of criticism as to why inmates did not appear to become rehabilitated, applauded the measure.

137

Prisoners, too, supported Senate Bill 42.[4] Many liberals, however, were not pleased at the disappearance of rehabilitation as a primary goal of imprisonment. The California State Bar Committee on Criminal Justice issued a document entitled "Report and Recommendations on Sentencing and Prison Reform," which summarizes the arguments of both sides. The majority of attorneys on the committee felt that the indeterminate sentence should be retained and serious and adequate rehabilitative efforts made, since in the past the state and prison administrators did not really try to rehabilitate.[5] The majority of the committee felt that fixed terms do not consider the wide differences in individual prisoners, that they are equally arbitrary and remove all incentive for prisoners to change.[6] The majority recommended that the California parole boards for men and women be abolished and release decisions be made by hearing officers independent of the prison administration. (This is what parole boards were supposed to be.)

The minority opinion supported the concept of fixed sentences. They agreed with the majority that rehabilitative efforts have been inadequate and that parole boards have been operating a vast network of administrative "courts" that proceeded unfairly and ineffectively. They agreed that rehabilitation should be a goal of imprisonment. However, their decision to support Senate Bill 42 was based on the desperate need for immediate reform.[7] They pointed out that the indeterminate sentence

... proceeds from a theory that prisoners will be released when they are rehabilitated. At present, California prisons do not make aggressive efforts to rehabilitate; they are not staffed with experts in rehabilitation; they do not possess the techniques sufficient for rehabilitation; and they are not budgeted for rehabilitation. . . .[8]

The minority report also points out that the rate of recidivism among those who were never paroled, but were discharged from prison upon completion of the maximum sentence, was statistically the same as those selected for release by the parole board, and that the parole board could not successfully predict recidivism in individual cases.[9] The minority opinion argued that the injustices committed must be stopped *immediately*. Rehabilitation was slow in coming; in fact, not much of a real rehabilitative nature was ever instituted in prisons. Thus, the call for more rehabilitation is unrealistic. The state is unable to finance the needed heavy commitment to rehabilitation, because of its already heavy financial commitments, the huge increase in unemployment and welfare rolls, and the decrease in tax revenues. The minority believed that the trial judge was better equipped than parole boards to fix sentences. Ultimately, the fixing of sentences was a legislative responsibility, not that of a group of bureaucrats unexposed to the public. The minority concluded:

At a future date, determinate sentencing may be inappropriate. Today it is badly needed. In an enlightened time, rehabilitation techniques will be better developed and the causes of crime will be understood. When that enlightened time arrives, indeterminate sentencing may again be the best approach.[10]

The minority opinion has become the law. The Nejedly bill allows the judge to choose from a range of narrow sentences, so narrow that gross disparities should be impossible. Under the new bill, the sentencing judge will be required to choose the middle sentence in each category unless the defense has presented evidence supporting a minimum sentence, or the prosecutor has presented evidence supporting a recommendation that the seriousness of the crime warrants the maximum sentence. For minor crimes, times to be served range between 16 months (minimum), 2 years (medium), and 3 years (maximum). For more serious crimes, sentences would extend from a minimum of 5 years, a middle range of 6 years, to a maximum of 7 years. While removing much of the uncertainty that has plagued inmates and corrections personnel alike, there is still the possibility of mitigating one's sentence. "Good time" can be earned so up to one-third of an inmate's sentence can be reduced. This "good time" can be earned by good conduct and by participation in rehabilitation activities. On the other hand, terms must be supplemented by additional time of up to three years for a history of the use of firearms, bodily injury, or violence. The new law is said to offer certainty of punishment upon conviction, along with the opportunity for rehabilitation if the convict wants to work for it. Under the Nejedly bill, the men's and women's parole boards are abolished and a new state agency to administer sentences, good time credit, and parole is established.

In the *Outlaw*, the journal of the Prisoners Union, prisoners point out why they supported the Nejedly bill.[11] First, some men and women were serving different amounts of time for commission of the same crime. Then, too, they point out that no one can say with reasonable accuracy when a person is "rehabilitated" or ready to be released from prison. Too often, "release readiness" was determined by a person's connections, background, attitude, or a change in the political climate and thus a change in sentencing policy. Prisoners support equitable sentences for everyone. Second, uncertainty about when an inmate would be released created more anxiety, frustration, bitterness, and violence. Third, under the indeterminate sentence, terms in California lengthened to where they are among the longest served anywhere in the world, far in excess of the recommendations of established groups such as the National Council on Crime and Delinquency, the President's Commission on Correctional Standards and Goals, and the National Advisory Commission on Criminal Justice. The element of the Nejedly bill that bothers prisoners the most is the fact that sentences imposed are still longer than those that studies have recommended. Fourth, decisions about release were made without procedural due process, in light of all relevant evidence and arguments, and instead were made through the arbitrary exercise of power.

The Prisoners Union feels that the fixed sentences under the Nejedly bill will alleviate the most immediate concerns of inmates. Under the bill, inmates will know exactly when they will be released. Conservatives and corrections personnel are pleased by the bill because it gives them more control over the whole sentencing and release process and also harsher sentencing of "criminals." And liberals? The rhetoric of rehabilitation sounded very humanistic and concerned about people's lives. However, abstracted from the actual practice of rehabilitation within the material conditions of life in the United States, the whole issue is meaningless. How was rehabilitation actually used in prisons? What kinds of positions are available in the larger society for ex-prisoners to go to? What kinds of jobs were prisoners being rehabilitated to perform? With unemployment at a high level, where is there room for over 1.5 million potential parolees? The state is in a fiscal crisis.[12] How is it possible for more funding to be given to prisons for rehabilitation activities? These are some of the material conditions ignored by liberal thinkers. In fact, the material conditions that supported liberal ideals of rehabilitation appear to have disappeared.

The research and political changes noted in this book indicate that, indeed, the goal of the National Council on Crime and Delinquency (NCCD) and the U.S. Board of Parole to make their implicit policy explicit has been achieved. What has happened in California is similar to what occurred on the federal level. The explicit policy of the U.S. Board of Parole corresponds to the new political reality. Board practices that would not have been legitimate several years ago are legitimate now. The implicit policy of the parole board to focus on offense severity and a corresponding amount of time to be served in determining an individual's sentence has become explicit policy. Seen historically, beginning with the NCCD study of parole decision making in 1970, we have a good indication of the trend that has been occurring in punishment policy. Recognizing that in the early 1970s economic conditions also began to deteriorate, we can see that political policy reflects and responds to material changes. This illustrates the fact that there are no immutable, eternal principles of social organization, but, rather, that social institutions are historical products that emerge and change dialectically through contradictions on the political, economic, and ideological levels. What appears to have occurred is the disappearance of rehabilitation as a goal of imprisonment in light of changed material conditions. With this disappearance and reduced emphasis on corrections, the problems and tasks of parole boards have also diminished, along with the need for such agencies.

Many years ago, Georg Rusche and Otto Kirchheimer analyzed the structure of penal practices historically from the perspective of dialectical materialism.[13] After discussing methods of punishment during various historical eras, they summed up their conclusions:

Every system of production tends to discover punishments which correspond to its productive relationships. It is thus necessary to investigate the origin and fate of penal systems, the use or avoidance of specific punishments, and the intensity of penal practices as they are determined by social forces, above all by economic and then fiscal forces.[14]

Punishment has historically been for either retribution or correction. The dominance of one or the other of these purposes has varied according to both the mode of production[15] and the condition of the labor market. As the relative surplus population increases, punishment becomes more retributive and corrections less important. For example, under feudalism, when there was a need for a greater laboring population, punishment was relatively light and corrections toward social utility of labor power of greater importance. Once the capacity of feudalism to support a growing population declined, punishments became harsher, functioning to remove the surplus population through corporal and capital punishment.[16] With the transition from feudalism to capitalism, the initial problem was to increase the supply of labor to meet the needs of the new mode of production. Policy, combined with enlightenment ideology, resulted in "houses of correction," designed to integrate criminals into the economy and make use of all possible labor power. As the labor supply reached desirable levels, punishment functioned once again as retribution rather than corrections. Thus, to understand the particular forms penal sanctions have taken, it is necessary to see them as historical processes that emerge and disappear as corresponding changes take place in the larger social order. Economic crises have historically led to an intensification of punishment.[17]

Historically, as a result of surplus population, attempts to find a rational policy of rehabilitation have been abandoned, but this has been concealed with a moral ideology.[18] Today this moral ideology includes the rhetoric that fixed sentencing is more humane and serves to alleviate prisoners' frustrations, which are assumed to arise from not knowing how much time they are to serve in prison. Part of this moral ideology also suggests that the indeterminate sentence was based on mistaken beliefs that offenders could be rehabilitated and that their future conduct could be predicted with some assurance of accuracy. Both of these understandings are said to be errors that must be corrected. Rather than instituting real rehabilitative programs, a recognized impossibility under the present organization of society, policy makers have abandoned the rhetoric of rehabilitation and chosen the path of fixed sentences, under the guise of a moral and humanitarian commitment and concern for prisoners.[19]

The practice of parole has consisted of having inmates serve specific periods of time in prison according to the kind of crime they committed. The practice has not changed but, rather, is now openly declared. Implicit policy has become explicit, legitimated and institutionalized by legislative action. Prison sentences, already too long, have been made even longer. The mechanisms of social control are tightening up, illustrative of the way in which intensification of punishment is a response to deteriorating social and economic conditions.

It is not the intent here to criticize liberal reforms. Those reforms which help to ameliorate the conditions under which people live are very important and should be supported. However, it is not certain that reforms such as determinate sentences and punishment instead of rehabilitation are liberal reforms or steps forward. Rationalized and clearly specified determinate sentences provide for greater social control over the whole process of release from prison. We cannot conceptualize and criticize "rehabilitation" in the abstract. Obviously, "rehabilitation" under these specific historical and material conditions left too much to the arbitrary power of parole boards and was an ideological tool but never a practice of prison institutions. However, under the guidelines and determinate sentences, inmates will be serving more time in prison. There may be no recourse under determinate sentences at all. It remains to be seen whether such reforms actually do make prison life easier.

The fate of punishment and parole is inexorably tied to the further development of capitalism. As Max Weber wrote long ago:

No one knows who will live in this cage in the future, or whether at the end of this tremendous development entirely new prophets will arise, or there will be a great rebirth of old ideas and ideals, or, if neither, mechanized petrification, embellished with a sort of convulsive self-importance. For the last stage of this cultural development, it might well be truly said: "Specialists without spirit, sensualists without heart; this nullity imagines that it has attained a level of civilization never before achieved.[20]

Author's Note: Late in 1976, the Board of Parole (now known as the Parole Commission) issued a new statement of its Rules and Regulations which modified its "scientifically" developed guidelines (*Federal Register*, 41, 173, Sept. 3, 1976:37316-17). Ranges of the amount of time to be served in nine categories were simply extended, allegedly because "the public welfare would best be protected by increased periods of incarceration for certain prisoners . . ." Changes in offense severity ratings were also made. For example, "immigration law violations" was increased from low to low/moderate severity to "provide adequate deterrence" to the influx of Mexican aliens. To combat potential political activism, the offense of possession and transportation of explosives was increased to high severity. Marijuana offenses were reduced in severity, reflecting changes in the law. These changes in the guidelines support the conclusion that amounts of time to be served and severity of the offense are determined by political considerations rather than any scientific data indicating that longer sentences have any effect, or that crimes are inherently more or less serious than thought before.

The salient factor score sheet, too, has undergone a process of erosion (*Federal Register*, 41, 233, Dec. 2, 1976:52890). The board has proposed to eliminate the items relating to educational background (Item G) and release plans (Item I) because education has "weak predictive value" and living arrangement is "difficult to score reliably." The board says that the revised device will "more accurately reflect the facts of each case in the areas selected for measurement" and "provide for more consistent decision-making." Not only are two items to be eliminated, but categories within the remaining items are also to be changed. It would be interesting to hear what the NCCD has to say.

The new extended time periods, changes in severity ratings, and revision of the salient factor score sheet reflect today's trend and legitimation of more punishment and more retribution as a simplistic solution for dealing with those already under fire.

Notes

Introduction

1. Positivism will be understood as an approach that is nonreflexive, chiefly concerned with "methodology," assumes science to be objective and "value-free," assumes conditions as given in the official version of reality, and favors existing arrangements in the current social order.

2. See, for example, Glaser, Daniel, "A Reconsideration of Some Parole Prediction Factors," *American Sociological Review*, Vol. 19, No. 3, June 1954, 335-341. Or they created mathematical models of "fairness" and "justice" and discussed these concepts in ahistorical vacuums as abstract Socratic puzzles. (Wilkins, L., "Foreword—Some Philosophical Issues—Values and the Parole Decision," *Parole Decision-Making: Supplemental Report Nine*, National Council on Crime and Delinquency, June 1973, xi-xix.)

3. Lest the foregoing sound as if criminologists and bureaucrats have gotten together to perpetrate some vicious conscious plot to misuse "science" to control or remove poor and powerless groups of people in support of the ruling class, it is important to recognize inherent structural imperatives and the impact of ideology, as well as the class position of most criminologists and upper level state bureaucrats such as parole board members. The class origins of these functionaries are primarily petty bourgeois. These people (primarily men) have come from family and class backgrounds where they have experienced more of the benefits offered by the existing system than most working people, or, at least, they have come from groups where the appearance of benefits received is more easily maintained. Thus, they take many existing ideological concepts as given. These agents have not experienced what the objects of their study or processing have had to undergo. As Richard Lichtman has pointed out, "The channeling of interpreted meaning is class structured. It is formed through lived engagement in the predominant class-controlled institutions of the society. . . . Those institutions which . . . pattern the development of socially shared meaning . . . are under the predominant control of that class of men who exercise hegemony over the means of production, distribution, exchange and consumption upon which society vitally depends." ("Symbolic Interactionism and Social Reality," *Berkeley Journal of Sociology*, Vol. 15, 1970) The mystification of professional academics and their service to the corporate order result from the ideological understandings they have internalized and their personal and class motivations. (See Schwendinger, H. and J., *Sociologists of the Chair*, New York: Basic Books, 1974, for a discussion of corporate business control as the primary source of mainstream sociological ideas.)

Both criminologists and bureaucrats are employees. They are chosen for institutions based on how well they will fit in with what the institutions were

143

intended to do. Criminologists and upper level bureaucrats are in positions where they are vulnerable, and they are therefore responsive to political pressures from above. For example, the status and salary of a professor are relatively low and it is often difficult to support a family; therefore, criminologists look for grants to keep them going and also to develop their careers. Grants are, as has been documented, given by those agencies and to those persons engaged in research supporting the established order. (See Quinney, R., *Critique of Legal Order*, Boston: Little, Brown, 1974.) The education of a criminologist does not emphasize political training or an understanding of power struggles or the fact that meaning is class structured. Most students in academia who have reached graduate level and those who become professors have little contact with working people and insurgent groups, and do not know what their lives and struggles are about.

The Schwendingers (*Sociologists of the Chair*) have developed a critical understanding of the interrelationship between the activities of professional sociologists who have analyzed problematic populations, and the corporate liberal state. Traditional sociologists throughout the history of North American sociology have legitimated the oppressive nature of many social institutions. Sociologists have been the "hired heads" of the corporate liberal order. These producers of ideology are very often more mystified than workers about the social processes in which they are involved. Thus, "human action can be understood neither independently of the meaning which the actor gives it, nor simply identified with his own interpretation. Recognition of the false consciousness of the actor is necessary to comprehend the nature of his acts. Activity has an objective structure which is often discrepant with its intended meaning" (Lichtman, "Symbolic Interactionism").

4. Glaser, Daniel, "Dialogue with Daniel Glaser, *Issues in Criminology*, Vol. 7, No. 2, 1972, 26. The book referred to is *The Effectiveness of a Prison and Parole System*, Indianapolis: Bobbs-Merrill, 1964.

5. Conrad, John, "Decisions, Decisions, Decisions," Address presented at the American Congress of Correction, Miami, 1971, in U.S. Department of Justice, *Parole Decision-Making: a Progress Report*, January 1973, 73-74.

6. Gottfredson, D. et al., *Parole Decision-Making: Summary*, National Council on Crime and Delinquency, June 1973, 42.

7. The method of *dialectical materialism* is defined as follows. Dialectical thought sees the world in perpetual motion, in terms of its internal conflicts and contradictions. No phenomenon can be seen in isolation from its interdependence with other larger phenomena, and must be evaluated from the standpoint of the historical conditions that gave rise to it over time. Social forms and social problems must be seen as a historical development that emerged through conflict between different social classes. In opposition to "idealism," which stresses the role of ideas in creating and maintaining the social world, "materialism" sees

social formations as arising from changes in the forces and relations of production and the clash of contradictions originating therefrom. Human behavior, motivation and ideas are not seen as abstract and static entities, but rather, in their interdependence with the way in which people produce and reproduce their existence.

In using dialectical materialism to understand various phenomena within the field of criminology, such as the parole process, it is necessary to be both historically specific and to see the phenomena in their interrelationship with the total social, political, and economic organization of society. Social relations are created by the political and economic structure. Criminal behavior can be understood as emerging within the capitalist system, as a result of the contradictions inherent in that structure of social relations. The most fundamental feature of people's lives is their relationship to the mode of production. Crime is the inevitable expression of class conflict in a society where economic relations are inherently exploitative. In a capitalist society, class conflict between the owners of the means of production and those who have nothing to sell but their labor power, results in various forms of criminal activity, as well as various forms of social control designed to eradicate or at least contain such behavior, to reproduce the same economic, political, and social relationships of power. People we commonsensically know as "criminals" come from those groups who threaten the social relations of production and thereby the position and domination of those who rule based upon their ownership of the means of production.

As Marx pointed out,

With the extension of the scale of production, and the mass of the labourers set in motion, with the greater breadth and fullness of all sources of wealth, there is also an extension of the scale on which greater attraction of labourers by capital is accompanied by their greater repulsion. . . . The labouring population therefore produces, along with the accumulation of capital produced by it, the means by which itself is made relatively superfluous, . . . and it does this to an always increasing extent. (Marx, Karl, *Capital*, N.Y.: International Publishers, 1967, 631)

Thus, the creation of a surplus population is an inherent contradiction in the capitalist mode of production. An excess population is necessary for the continued accumulation of capital and exploitation of workers for profit, but such populations are potentially dangerous and revolutionary. "Criminals" form a large portion of that surplus population, and are thus a very threatening group upon which a great deal of money must be spent in containment and control. Those who commit "street crimes" come primarily from this class of persons. Their activity is rationally understood as a reaction to their limited economic opportunities and low-class position in the social structure. "White-collar crime," as well as "organized crime" are rational kinds of activities within the structure of capitalist relations. For example, why should people work for a subsistence-level wage, when they are told to consume and see others consuming, and when it is possible to make much more money doing something else for which there is a high demand. Crime performs valuable functions for the capitalist society, in providing an outlet or alternative means of upward mobility for otherwise dependent and dangerous groups. Thus, crime reduces the surplus population by creating employment for groups that otherwise would have none, and creating jobs for a variety of bureaucrats involved in institutions of social control. Crime also helps to pacify problematic populations, through the provision of drugs, sex, and gambling to alleviate the pains and frustrations of life in capitalist society, and diverts people's attention from the exploitation they experience in their daily life. The structure of competition creates the need on the part of capitalists themselves to protect and continue to accumulate large amounts of capital, for capitalism does not provide for any real economic security.

All classes in capitalist society engage in criminal activity. The forms vary depending on an individual's class position and opportunities and on the kind of socialization experience he or she has undergone. It is in the enforcement of the law that crime becomes a lower class phenomenon. There are few consequences for those who engage in white-collar or corporate crime. The ruling class exercises tight control over who will be processed through the "criminal justice" system. The criminal law is thus not a "reflection of custom," nor based on any agreed-upon consensus or agreement among various comparative interest groups. It is a set of rules created by those who rule in their own interests, and is a result of the inherent contradictions and ensuing struggles in class societies.

For a further discussion of these issues, see: Quinney, Richard, *Critique of Legal Order*, Boston: Little, Brown, 1974; Spitzer, Steven, "Towards a Marxian Theory of Deviance," *Social Problems*, Vol. 22, No. 5, June 1975, 638-651; Gordon, David, "Class and the Economics of Crime," *Review of Radical Political Economy*, Vol. 3, No. 3, Summer 1971; Chambliss, William, "Toward a Political Economy of Crime," *Theory and Society*, 1975; Manders, Dean, "Labelling Theory and Social Reality: A Marxist Critique," *The Insurgent Sociologist*, Vol. VI, No. 1, Fall 1975, 53-66.

Chapter 1
Theory and Practice of Parole

1. A few days taken off an inmate's sentence every month for "good behavior"; for a long-term prisoner this may amount to ten days a month (18 U.S.C. 4161).

2. *Parole* is defined as "serving a portion of one's sentence outside of prison under supervision of state authorities." In effect, regular sentences are also indeterminate sentences because most releases are by parole after some minimum time is served.

3. See Miller, Martin, "The Indeterminate Sentence Paradigm," *Issues in Criminology*, Vol. 7, No. 2, Fall 1972, 116.

4. *Ideology* is defined as the way we have been socialized by the dominant institutions to perceive and interpret our lived social relations.

5. Taylor, I. et al., *The New Criminology*, New York: Harper & Row, 1973, 1-10.

The classical view of crime developed out of the philosophy of the Enlightenment in the eighteenth century. Its assumptions and theses are the same as those embodied in liberal theory of the laissez-faire variety. What is known as classical theory was first formulated by the Italian Cesare Beccaria, based on the social contract theories of Hobbes and Rousseau. Beccaria argued that

Laws are the conditions under which men, naturally independent, united themselves in society. Weary of living in a continual state of war and of enjoying a liberty which became of little value, from the uncertainty of its duration, they sacrificed one part of it, to enjoy the rest in peace and security. The sum of all these portions of the liberty of each individual constituted the sovereignty of a nation; and was deposited in the hands of the sovereign, as the lawful administrator. But it was not sufficient only to establish this deposit; it was also necessary to defend it from the usurpation of each individual, who would always endeavour not only to take away from the mass his own portion, but to encroach on that of others." (Beccaria, C., (1804) "Essays on Crimes and Punishments," in H. Mannheim, ed., *Pioneers in Criminology*, London: Stevens, 1960)

Beccaria could not help but note, however, that criminality was more concentrated in the "dangerous, unpropertied class."

He who endeavours to enrich himself with the property of another, should be deprived of part of his own. But this crime, alas! is commonly the effect of misery and despair; the crime of that unhappy part of mankind, to whom the right of exclusive property (a terrible and perhaps unnecessary right) has left but a bare existence. (Ibid)

Classical theorists avoided discussion of this contradiction, which throws doubt on the justice of the "social contract" itself. Another classical theorist, John Locke, made a distinction between the poor who chose depravity and those who, because of unfortunate circumstances, could not live a rational life. However, he too evaded the essential contradiction. Classical theory focused on the legal and penal systems and not the motivations of the criminal actor. Today, the classical view of crime is embodied in the theoretical writings of Edward Banfield (*The Unheavenly City*, Boston: Little, Brown, 1968), who also bases his argument on the assumption that individuals have the free choice to commit or not commit crimes, but choose to do so based upon rational calculation of costs and rewards. Banfield's theory assumes that there is natural inequality, and that the natural abilities of the more fit members of a society enable them to rise to the top and take over the operation of society, while those who are less able fall to the bottom. The less fit members are the lower classes, who cannot conform or adapt themselves to the socially agreed-upon existing structure but, rather, interfere with its smooth running. "Degenerates" are only interested in immediate gratification and overly indulgent of their animal instincts. Poverty, and thus criminal activity, result from one's orientation to the future and not from class position, structured inequalities, or differential power relationships. The policy implications of his theory are that greater social control is necessary so costs become greater than rewards. The only effective way to compel someone not to commit a crime is to lock him up.

6. Although the positivist approach is today reactionary in the service of the status quo, positivism is not inherently so. It was at one time a progressive conceptualization of the world, of knowledge, and of learning. In Europe during the late sixteenth and seventeenth centuries, positivism emerged as a protest movement against the narrow formalism and authoritarian definitions that prevailed under the domination of the Catholic Church, the ruling aristocracy, and the Scholastics. Early positivists, such as François Rabelais, Michel de Montaigne, and Francis Bacon, argued that knowledge came from practical and sensory experience with the real, natural world, rather than from books written by dead authors, rote memorization, and acceptance of religious dogma. The answer to understanding human behavior lay in the natural world, not in the classical humanities or religious creeds. Nature's secrets could be revealed by an accumulation of facts, direct study, objective verification, and mathematical analysis. This was the "scientific method." Many positivists attacked corrupt representatives of powerful medieval institutions and ridiculed traditional ideas and practices. The plan of Francis Bacon was that after the mind was rid of "idols" or preconceptions, lists of all the facts of nature could be gathered and tabulated through the cooperative effort of scientists and inventors, and this kind of scientific organization would result in the dominance of human power over the environment. Bacon saw ideas as blocking the way; if new ideas could replace old ones, mankind could advance. Bacon unfortunately did not see these ideas as shaped by material existence. Although early positivists emphasized critical reasoning and a questioning attitude, and saw the world as operating according to "natural laws" that could be discovered, rather than according to the whims of an unknown God, they theorized in ahistorical vacuums. They did not delineate the specific conditions of power based on the process of production through which existence was maintained. Arising at a historical period when capitalism was replacing feudalism, when the "scientific method" was a valuable ideological and technical tool for capitalist development, positivism was harnessed in the service of the bourgeoisie.

One of the early positivists who related the "scientific method" to crime was Enrico Ferri (*The Positivist School of Criminology*, Chicago: C. Kerr, 1908), who saw the mission of a science of society as eradicating crime. Positivists were interested in the psychological and environmental reasons why an individual failed to internalize the norms of a system the majority were presumed to accept. The focus of criminology as a science was on the criminal actor rather than the criminal law. Positivists, such as Raffaele Garofalo (*Criminology*, Boston: Little, Brown, 1914), searched for a definition of "natural crime" independent of the legal system, in terms of injury to some high moral sense. The most elaborate development of the theory of the natural born criminal was in the works of Cesare Lombroso (*L'Uomo Delinquente*, Torino: Bocca, 1897). The secret of criminality was found in biological and physical differences between criminals and normals. Lombroso theorized:

Today there is a vague feeling, an echo of an ancient retaliation in our punishments. If punishment rests on free will, the worse men, the criminals by nature, should have a very light punishment or none. Penal repressions should be based on social utility scientifically demonstrated; instead of studying law texts, we need to study the criminal. The criminal by nature has a feeble cranial capacity, a heavy and developed jaw, a large orbital capacity, projecting superciliary ridges, an abnormal and symmetrical cranium, a scanty beard or none, but abundant hair, projecting ears, frequently a crooked or flat nose. Criminals are subject to Daltonism: left-handedness, is common; their muscular force is feeble. Alcoholic and epileptical degeneration exists in a large number. Their nerve centers are frequently pigmented. They blush with difficulty. Their moral degeneration corresponds with their physical, their criminal tendencies are manifested in infancy by onanism, cruelty, inclination to steal, excessive vanity, impulsive character. The criminal by nature is lazy, debauched, cowardly, not susceptible to remorse, without foresight, fond of tatooing; his handwriting is peculiar, signature complicated and adorned with flourishes; his slang is widely diffused, abbreviated and full of archaisms. In their associations they return to primitive social forms. The general cause of the persistence of an inferior race type is atavistic. As the born criminal is without remedy, he must be continually confined, and allowed no provisional liberty or mercy. (Quoted in Platt, Anthony, *The Child Savers*, Chicago: University of Chicago Press, 1965, 21-22)

The theories of Lombroso were popular because they confirmed prevailing assumptions about the existence of a "criminal class" that could be scientifically distinguished from noncriminals and thus eradicated.

Other positivists developed a tradition of sociological rather than biological positivism, taking into account social factors that influenced criminal activity. A. Quetelet (*Treatise on Man*, Paris: Bachelier, 1842) and A. Guerry (*Statistique Morale...*, 1863, in Radzinowicz, L. *Ideology and Crime*, London: Heinemann, 1966) attempted to deal with crime as a social phenomenon, noting that crime statistics remained relatively consistent and that crime was a regular feature of social order rather than the product of individual propensities. Some fundamental features of existing social arrangements gave rise to regular criminal outcomes, and, therefore, science could come to specify the causes of this and thus eliminate the phenomenon. Such works provided the foundation for the theories of Emile Durkheim a few years later. However, the appeal of biological positivism was stronger and served the material and ideological interests of the powerful. The ideas of Lombroso predominated over those of Guerry and Quetelet. There are dangerous implications in the idea that crime is the product of social organization.

7. For example, George Lundberg, president of the American Sociological Association in 1944, ascribed social disasters to the fact that the social sciences were not as developed as the physical sciences (Mills, C.W., "The Powerless People," *Politics*, Vol. 1, April 1944, 68).

8. Dressler, David, *Practice and Theory of Probation and Parole*, New York: Columbia University Press, 1959, 44.

9. See testimony of Leonard Orland, *Hearings before Subcommittee No. 3 of the Committee on the Judiciary*, House of Representatives, 92nd Congress, Session II, 1972, on H.R. 13118 and Related Bills, Part VII-A, Serial No. 15, p. 85.

10. The issue of treatment and rehabilitation is not the focus of this study and has been examined in great detail elsewhere. See, for example, Irwin, John, *The Felon*, Boston: Little, Brown, 1974; American Friends Service Committee, *Struggle for Justice*, New York: Hill and Wange, 1971; Robison, J., and Smith, G., "The Effectiveness of Correctional Programs," *Crime and Delinquency*, January 1971, 67-80. (See also footnote 35.)

11. Through trial and error, inmates come to know what the parole board expects from them; they learn the language of the "cured," and their real selves retreat behind façades. Only the negative elements have meaning. Positive reports do not speed up release, but negative reports can delay it. The kinds of questions asked during hearings give hints as to what the board is looking for, and other inmates who have appeared before the board give clues as to "normal" amounts of time people have served. See Miller, Martin, "The Indeterminate Sentence Paradigm," 114-116.

12. Recent controversies and criticism of the U.S. Board of Parole have caused its members to issue statements and guidelines that indicate factors they consider in making a parole decision.

13. *Hearings before Subcommittee No. 3*, p. 83.

14. Sage, Wayne, "Crime and the Clockwork Lemon," *Human Behavior*, September 1974, 16-24; Ingraham, B., and Smith, G., "The Use of Electronics in the Observation and Control of Human Behavior and its Possible Use in Rehabilitation and Parole," and Shapiro, M., "The Uses of Behavior Control Technologies," *Issues in Criminology*, Vol. 7, No. 2, fall 1972.

15. *Congressional Record*, 61st Congress, Session II, Chs. 386-87, 1910; *Congressional Record*, 71st Congress, Session II, Chs. 254-55, 1930; *U.S. Statutes at Large*, Vol. 36, Pt. 1, p. 819; Vol. 46, Pt. 1, p. 272.

16. *Hearings before the Committee on the Judiciary*, House of Representatives, 71st Congress, Session II, on H.R. 6807, 7410, 7411, 7412, 7413, 7832,

December 19, 1929, U.S. Government Printing Office, p. 12. It is no wonder, then, that labor in prison is useless in the outside world, with this concern over cheaper prison labor.

17. Atlanta, for example, with a normal capacity of 1,580, had a population of 8,687. Ibid., 12.

18. Ibid., 18-19. Later testimony by the superintendent of prisons indicated that the government recognized the cause of overcrowding as due to the enactment of new laws establishing new crimes that had not been crimes before. However, his comment was, ". . . we need not have any particular alarm over the situation . . . it does not mean that the country is any more criminal than it was before . . . it means we have changed to some extent our statutory methods of controlling crime" (p. 24).

19. Ibid., 26.

20. Ibid., 21.

21. U.S. Board of Parole, *Biennial Report*, 1968 to 1970, 1970 to 1972.

22. *Functions of the U.S. Board of Parole*, Washington, D.C., p. 2.

23. U.S. Board of Parole, *Rules and Regulations*, June 5, 1974.

24. Hoffman, P., and Gottfredson, D., *Parole Decision-Making; Supplemental Report, No. 9, Paroling Policy Guidelines: A Matter of Equity*, National Council on Crime and Delinquency, June 1973, 8.

25. Johnson, P., *Federal Parole Procedures*, Administrative Conference of the United States, January 1972, 6.

26. *Hearings before Subcommittee No. 3*, 92.

27. Ibid., 385.

28. U.S. Board of Parole, *Rules and Regulations*, Section 2.18. There is no statutory criterion relating to treatment and rehabilitation.

29. Davis, Kenneth C., *Discretionary Justice*, Baton Rouge: Louisiana University Press, 1969, 127.

30. U.S. Board of Parole, *Biennial Report*, 21-22.

31. The federal courts have refused to intervene with the discretion of the parole board to grant or deny parole. See, for example, *Juelich vs. U.S. Board of Parole*, 437 F.2d 1147 (7th Cir. 1971); *Thompkins vs. Board of Parole*, 427 F.2d 222 (5th Cir. 1970); *U.S. vs. Frederick*, 405 F.2d 129 (3rd Cir. 1968); *Schwartzenberger vs. U.S. Board of Parole*, 399 U.S. Board of Parole, 399 U.S. 297 (10th Cir. 1968); *Brest vs. Ciccone*, 371 F.2d 981 (8th Cir. 1967).

32. However, the courts have not precluded intervention regarding specific procedural reforms derived from the Administrative Procedure Act, the Constitution, and so on. In October 1974 the board's new guidelines were declared void because of noncompliance with administrative procedures regarding advance public notice of rule making and public participation therein. The board claims such rule making is related to internal agency organization and not

subject to these procedures. See case of *Pickus vs. U.S. Board of Parole*, CA DC, October 11, 1974, summary in 16 CrL 2080-2082, October 23, 1974. The board is appealing the decision.

33. Under the new rules, an inmate may have a representative at the hearing who may make a statement on his behalf.

34. See case of Olivia Sanchez in Appendix 1A.

35. See footnote 10 and Cressey, D., "Limitations of Treatment," in N. Johnson et al., eds., *The Sociology of Punishment and Correction*, New York: John Wiley & Sons, 1970, 501-508; Mitford, J., *Kind and Unusual Punishment*, New York: Random House, 1974; Korn, R., and McKorkle, L., "Resocialization within Walls," *Annals of the Academy of Political and Social Sciences*, 293, May 1954, 88-98; Lefcourt, R. *Law Against the People*, New York: Random House, 1971; Wright, Erik, *The Politics of Punishment*, New York: Harper & Row, 1973; Manocchio, A., and Dunn, J., *The Time Game*, New York: Dell, 1970; Goffman, E., *Asylums*, New York: Doubleday, 1961; Quinney, R., *Critique of Legal Order*, Boston: Little, Brown, 1974; Lipton, D. et al., *The Effectiveness of Correctional Treatment*, New York: Praeger, 1975.

36. Warner, S.B., "Factors Determining Parole from the Massachusetts Reformatory," *Journal of Criminal Law and Criminology*, 14, 1923, 172-207; Testimony of Dr. Willard Gaylin, *Hearings before Subcommittee No. 3*, 447; Stanley, David, *Prisoners Among Us: The Problem of Parole*, Washington, D.C.: Brookings Institute, 1976, Ch. 4.

37. See testimony of Dr. Leonard Orland and Dr. Willard Gaylin, *Hearings before Subcommittee No. 3*.

38. Testimony of Dr. Willard Gaylin, *Hearings before Subcommittee No. 3*, 450.

39. Ibid., 450. For example, "X is making a good adjustment. However, whether he is paroled should be in keeping with the Board's current policy governing this type of offense."

Appendix 1A
Criteria for Parole

1. Warner, S.B., "Factors Determining Parole . . . ," *Journal of Criminal Law and Criminology*, Vol. 14, 1923, 172-207;
    Hart, H., "Predicting Parole Success," *General Criminal Law and Criminology*, Vol. 14, 1923, 405-413;
    Burgess, E.W., in Bruce, A., Burgess, E. and Harno, A., *The Working of the Indeterminate Sentence Law in the Parole System in Illinois*, Springfield, 1928, Chapters 28 to 30;
    Glueck, S., and Glueck, E., *Five Hundred Criminal Careers*, New York:

Knopf, 1930; *Five Hundred Delinquent Women; One Thousand Juvenile Delinquents*; and several other works;

Vold, G.B., *Prediction Methods and Parole*, New Hampshire: Sociological Press, 1931;

Monachesi, E.D., *Prediction Factors in Probation*, New Hampshire: Sociological Press, 1932;

Tibbits, C., "Success and Failure in Parole Can Be Predicted," *Journal of Criminal Law, Criminology and Police Science*, 1931, 22;

Attorney General's Survey of Release Procedures, 4: Parole, Washington, D.C.: Department of Justice, 1939;

Ohlin, L., *Selection for Parole*, New York: Russell Sage Foundation, 1951;

Reiss, A.J., "The Accuracy, Efficiency and Validity of a Prediction Instrument," *American Journal of Sociology*, May 1951, 61;

Dunham, R., "Factors Related to Recidivism in Adults," *Journal of Social Psychology*, Vol. 39, 1954;

Glaser, D., "A Reconsideration of Some Parole Prediction Factors," *American Sociological Review*, 1954, 19;

Mannheim, H., and Wilkins, L., *Prediction Methods in Relation to Borstal Training*, London: Her Majesty's Stationery Office, 1955;

Simon, Frances, *Prediction Methods in Criminology*, London: Her Majesty's Stationery Office, 1972, Chapter 3;

Gottfredson, D., "Assessment and Prediction Methods in Crime and Delinquency," *Task Force Report: Juvenile Delinquency and Youth Crime*, the President's Commission on Law Enforcement and Administration of Justice, Washington, D.C., U.S. Government Printing Office, 1967.

2. Thomas, Paul, "Analysis of Parole Selection," *Crime and Delinquency*, Vol. 8, No. 2, 1962.

3. In effect, this more probably reflects the board's attempt to equalize the disparate sentences given by judges for similar offenses, rather than individual considerations.

4. *You and the Parole Board*, U.S. Board of Parole, January 1971.

5. Rules of the United States Board of Parole, 1971, 14-16.

6. Gottfredson, D. et al., *Parole Decision-Making: Summary*; "The Utilization of Experience in Parole Decision-Making: A Progress Report," Davis, California: NCCD, January 1973, 30-31.

7. Sigler, Maurice, Preface, *Parole Decision-Making: Supplemental Report Nine*, "Paroling Policy Guidelines: A Matter of Equity," Hoffman, P., and Gottfredson, D., Davis, California: NCCD, June 1973, vii.

8. U.S. Board of Parole, *Parole, Release, Supervision and Recommitment of Prisoners, Youth Offenders and Juvenile Delinquents: Rules and Regulations*, Department of Justice, June 5, 1974.

Chapter 2
The United States of America vs. David Donner

1. Fictitious names have been used in this chapter and others in discussing particular inmates and situations.

2. Selltiz, C. et al., *Research Methods in Social Relations*, New York: Henry Holt & Company, 1959, 59-64.

3. See Daniels, A.K., "The Social Construction of Military Psychiatric Diagnoses," *Recent Sociology, No. 2*, New York: Macmillan, 1970, 203-204, regarding the ways in which psychiatrists take into account situational contingencies such as the consequences of their actions and "needs" of the particular institutional system, when formulating a diagnosis.

4. See Appendix 1A: Criteria for Parole.

5. *Larceny* is defined by the FBI as the unlawful taking of property or articles of value *without* the use of force, violence, or fraud (*Crime in the U.S.*, Washington, D.C.: Department of Justice, 1970). This raises the whole issue of the purpose of plea bargaining.

6. Judges should therefore become aware that giving an individual an "a" number has no differential effect.

7. Use of this obscure statute occurs only rarely, and generally in cases of obvious innocence.

8. Case study methods are not standardized to permit comparisons of large groups. Biases of the researcher may affect the outcome to a greater extent than in statistical analyses of large samples. From one case, not chosen randomly, it is difficult to generalize and determine the significance of conclusions or broader application of the findings. Later researchers would have greater difficulty in replicating such a study, and predictive validity from the results would be uncertain.

Chapter 3
A Quantitative Analysis of Decision Making

1. A more extended discussion of this phenomenon will follow in a later chapter.

2. See Appendix 1A: Criteria for Parole.

3. See Appendix 3A for a brief description of the purposes underlying the gathering of this data.

See NCCD Reports on *Parole Decision-Making*, 1971-191 3:

One: Development of a Data Base for Parole Decision-Making
Two: Parole Decision-Making Coding Manual

4. The National Council on Crime and Delinquency (NCCD) devised several code sheets for recording information. These are on file with the author.

5. See Appendix 3A: Recoded Analysis Variables.

6. See Appendix 1A: Criteria for Parole.

7. Amos, W., Address Presented at American Congress of Correction, Florida, August 1971; Meehl, P., *Clinical vs. Statistical Prediction*, University of Minnesota Press, 1954.

8. Seriousness of offense is discussed in greater detail in Chapter 4. For now, "seriousness" is not recognized as ideological but, rather, as essential fact because of consensus among groups of persons tested. See Sellin, T., and Wolfgang, M., *The Measurement of Delinquency*, New York: John Wiley & Sons, 1964; Rossi, P. et al., "The Seriousness of Crimes: Normative Structure and Individual Differences," *American Sociological Review*, Vol. 37, No. 2, April 1974, 224-237; Blumstein, A., "Seriousness Weights in an Index of Crime," *American Sociological Review*, Vol. 39, No. 6, December 1974, 854-864; Warren, M., "Severity of Parolee Violation Behavior: An Instrument for Its Assessment," Master's Thesis, University of California, Berkeley, January 1964.

9. "Amount of time to be served" was said to be arrived at by calculating the median time served for sets of offense ratings (behavior descriptions of offenses). Offense ratings with similar median times served were combined to produce the six severity-level classifications. The median time served was tabulated for each severity level. Some "smoothing" occurred based on agreement between two NCCD-project staff members. The size of the range was determined after informal discussions with several board members and hearing examiners. We are told that the range size is arbitrary and only to some extent proportional to the size of the median. We are in effect led through a process of mystification as to how these time ranges were actually determined. This does not mean that there is a correlation between the time served and later success on

parole (NCCD Parole Decision-Making, Supplemental Report Nine, *Paroling Policy Guidelines: A Matter of Equity*, June 1973, 10-12).

10. See cases cited earlier of David Donner and Olivia Sanchez, and cases in Appendix 3A of Arthur Young, Robert Green, and Bill Gardner.

11. The sixth category, "greatest severity," was combined with "very high severity" because of the very small number of cases involved.

12. Mueller, J. et al., *Statistical Reasoning in Sociology*, Second Edition, Boston: Houghton-Mifflin, 1970, 249-254. Lambda may range from 0 to 1. A value of zero indicates that no reduction in error is achieved and that knowledge of the independent variable does not help at all in predicting the dependent variable. A value of 1 indicates that knowledge of the independent variable permits the prediction of the dependent variable without any error at all.

13. For all practical purposes, "continue to a fixed date for rehearing" constitutes a denial of parole. The board disagrees that this is so, and in reporting its activities in its biennial reports ignores individuals in this category and bases its percentages of parole on those paroled or continued to the expiration of their entire sentence. See *Biennial Reports*, 18-20, and see argument in *Hearings*, House of Representatives, 395-398.

14. See Appendix 1A: Criteria for Parole.

15. Appendix 3A: Recoded Analysis Variables describes in detail the data transformations from the NCCD study. See also NCCD Code Sheets themselves.

16. Andrews, F., and Messenger, R., *Multivariate Nominal Scale Analysis*, Survey Research Center, Institute for Social Research, Ann Arbor, Michigan: University of Michigan, 1973.

17. Andrews, F., Morgan, J., and Sonquist, J. *The Multiple Classification Analysis Program: A Report of a Computer Program*, Ann Arbor, Michigan: Institute for Social Research, 1967.

18. This is the same as the Lambda statistic discussed earlier.

19. Andrews F., and Messenger, R., *Multivariate Nominal Scale Analysis*, 11-15.

20. The coefficients and adjusted percents indicate the same phenomena. We are reporting effects in terms of the coefficients here.

21. This phenomenon is recognized by the board. "Persons sentenced to relatively short sentences and who have committed serious offenses are not likely to be paroled. On the other hand, those who are sentenced to unusually long terms may earn parole at some point in their sentence . . . the Board eventually paroles a high percentage of those prisoners who receive long sentences . . . in contrast to bank robbers, those convicted of immigration law violations receive parole only a small percent of the time. This is generally so because of the short sentence they receive. . . . Drug law offenders tend to receive parole rather frequently because of their long sentences. . . ." (U.S. Board of Parole, *Biennial Report*, 1968-70, 22)

22. The variables that appear not to matter here have probably had an effect earlier as the individuals were processed through the system by the police, social agencies, courts and prisons, and therefore they do affect the board in an indirect way, for example, by affecting prison custody classification or sentencing by the court. But they do not really help to explain the parole decision.

23. The formula for conversion is:

$$= \frac{\theta_1 - 0}{1 - \theta}$$

where θ is the modal category of the overall distribution of parole decision (Andrews, F., and Messenger, R., *Multivariate Nominal Scale Analysis*, 33, equation 3-28).

24. Irwin, John, *The Felon*, Englewood Cliffs, New Jersey: Prentice-Hall, 1970, 55.

Appendix 3A
NCCD Project and Parole Decision Making

1. Singer, S., and Gottfredson, D., *Parole Decision-Making: Supplemental Report One*, Davis, California: NCCD Research Center, June 1973, 1.

2. *Fairness* was defined in terms of a statistical model of uniform treatment of a specific large sample of like persons. See Wilkins, Leslie T., "Some Philosophical Issues—Values and the Parole Decision," *Parole Decision-Making: Supplemental Report Nine*, Davis, California: NCCD Research Center, June 1973, xi-xix.

3. Such limits set upon the researchers must also be limits the board faces in making its decisions to parole or deny.

4. See NCCD Code Sheets, Appendix 3A.

5. Beck, J. et al., *Parole Decision-Making: Supplemental Report No. 12*, NCCD, June 1973.

6. U.S. Board of Parole, *You and the Parole Board*, 5.

7. See, for example, Glaser, D., "A Reconsideration of Some Parole Prediction Factors," *American Sociological Review*, Vol. 19, No. 3, June 1954, 335-341. Glaser pointed out that parolees who were students or who worked steadily before their offense had a violation rate of only 24.4 percent as contrasted with 44.5 percent for those with unstable work records, almost double. This would indicate the importance of work as a factor in committing "crimes."

Chapter 4
The Political Economy of Parole

1. Wright, Erik, *The Politics of Punishment*, New York: Harper and Row, 1973, 127-131.

2. They probably would not have been allowed to, as the board guards its practices carefully.

3. See footnote 7, Introduction, for discussion of this method.

4. Mr. Justice Douglas, Supreme Court of the United States, Dissenting in part, *Morrissey v. Brewer*, 408 U.S. 471 (1972).

5. Studies have shown that providing jobs with interesting work and opportunities for advancement has been very successful in reducing recidivism. See, for example, Chaneles, Sol, "A Job Program for Ex-convicts that Works," *Psychology Today*, March 1975, 43-46.

6. Robischon, T., Rabow, J., and Schmidt, J., *Cracks in the Classroom Wall*, Pacific Palisades: Goodyear, 1974.

7. Foucault, Michel, "On Attica: An Interview," *Telos*, No. 19, Spring 1974, 155.

8. Ibid., 158. We can find many examples of this in studies of prisoners who have been released. See, for example, Burkhart, Kitsi, "Women in Prison," *Ramparts*, Vol. 9, No. 11, June 1971, 29.

9. Marx, Karl, *Capital*, I, Chicago: Charles Kerr & Co., 1933.

10. Ibid., 701.

11. For a discussion of the importance of the relative surplus population to various forms of deviance, created through the external contradictions of capitalism, see Spitzer, S., "Toward a Marxian Theory of Deviance," *Social Problems*, Vol. 22, No. 5, 1975, 638-651.

12. *Los Angeles Times*, July 22, 1975, I.

13. U.S. Bureau of Prisons Report, "Correlation of Unemployment and Federal Prison Population," March 1975.

14. Sutherland, E., and Cressey, D., *Principles of Criminology*, Chicago: J.B. Lippincott Co., 1960, 189.

15. Glueck, S. and E., *One Thousand Juvenile Delinquents*, Cambridge: Harvard University Press, 1934; *Five Hundred Criminal Careers*, New York: Knopf, 1930; *Five Hundred Delinquent Women*, New York: Knopf, 1934.

16. See, for example, Caldwell, M., "The Economic Status of Families of Delinquent Boys," *American Journal of Sociology*, Vol. 37, September 1931; Kvaraceus, W., "Juvenile Delinquency and Social Class," *Journal of Educational Sociology*, Vol. 18, September 1944; Shaw, C., and McKay, H., *Juvenile Delinquency and Urban Areas*, Chicago: University of Chicago Press, 1942, 141.

17. Ibid.

18. U.S. Department of Justice, Law Enforcement Assistance Administration, *Survey of Inmates of Local Jails: 1972.*

19. See, for example, *National Prisoner Statistics*, U.S. Bureau of Prisons, 1950, 1960. It is almost as if gathering data on economic status would be far too revealing of the bases built into the system.

20. For the NCCD sample population, approximately 50 percent (4,330) fell into category (a), 15 percent (1,259) into category (b), and 35 percent (3,080) into category (c). They pointed out that this item had a relatively low level of reliability because there was seldom sufficient information in the case file or it required computation by coders and was therefore open to error. However, they decided it did have predictive utility because the distinction between categories (b) and (c) was unimportant; what was important was whether the individual was gainfully employed for any length of time, and this generally showed up in the file.

21. U.S. Department of Justice, *Survey of Inmates of Local Jails*, 1.

22. Ares, C. et al., "The Manhattan Bail Project," in Johnston, N. et al., eds., *The Sociology of Punishment and Correction*, New York: John Wiley & Sons, 1962, 187-188.

23. Wright, Erik, *The Politics of Punishment*, New York: Harper & Row, 1973, 26.

24. See, for example, Boyer, R., and Morais, H., *Labor's Untold Story*, New York: United Electrical, Radio & Machine Workers of America, 1955; Center for Research on Criminal Justice, *The Iron Fist and the Velvet Glove*, Berkeley, 1975.

25. San Diego Street Journal, *Gimmee some Truth* (videotape), 1973, indicates the interrelationships among organized crime, right wing politics, and business. Also see Ianni, F., *Black Mafia*, New York: Pocket Books, 1973; Gordon, D., "Class and the Economics of Crime," *Review of Radical Political Economics*, Vol. 3, No. 3, Summer 1971, 51-75.

26. See Balbus, Isaac, *The Dialectics of Legal Repression*, New York: Russell Sage Foundation, 1973, for a discussion of the use of formal rationality to restore order and contain the revolutionary potential of ghetto struggles, as well as to achieve the long-term goal of legitimizing the structure of existing legal, political, economic, and social relations.

27. Althusser, Louis, "Ideology and Ideological State Apparatuses," *Lenin and Philosophy and Other Essays*, New York: Monthly Review Press, 1971, 137-158. For a discussion of the state, see also Engels F., *The Origin of the Family, Private Property and the State*, New York: International Publishers, 1942; Lenin, "The State and Revolution," *The Essential Left*, New York: Barnes & Noble, 1961; Miliband, Ralph, *The State in Capitalist Society*, New York: Basic Books, 1969.

28. Crime and Social Justice Collective, "The Politics of Street Crime," *Crime and Social Justice*, Vol. 5, Spring-Summer 1976, 1-4.

29. For a discussion of this issue, see Davis, Angela, *If They Come in the Morning*, New York: Joseph Okpaku, 1971, 19-38; and Wright, Erik, *The Politics of Punishment*, New York: Harper & Row, 1973, Chapter 2.

30. Although these crimes may be "rational" to the social scientist attempting to understand the behavior within the context of social conditions, the individual "criminal" may not necessarily be rationally aware of the conditions to which he is responding and his reaction may take an irrational form, such as in the crime of rape.

31. Robinson, J., and Smith, G., "The Effectiveness of Correctional Programs," *Crime and Delinquency*, January 1971, 71-72.

32. Ibid., 75.

33. Section 4203, Title 18, U.S. Code.

34. Conrad, John, "Decisions, Decisions, Decisions," Address presented at the American Congress of Correction, Miami, 1971, in U.S. Department of Justice, *Parole Decision-Making: A Progress Report*, January 1973, 67-68.

35. The probability of recidivism is viewed as the index of the extent to which the inmate has been rehabilitated, as well as a measure of the risk to society that his release would entail. See Dawson, R., "The Decision to Grant or Deny Parole," *Washington University Law Quarterly*, Vol. 1966, No. 3, June 1966, 249.

36. An example of positivist thinking is characterized by the following statement, "If attention were diverted from individual cases ("...his case was not fairly determined...") to questions of general principles of parole, the understanding and control of the system would, it seems, be increased in great measure. (See Gottfredson, D. et al., *Parole Decision-Making: Summary*, National Council on Crime and Delinquency, June 1973, 51.)

37. Of course, this is ideological, and in practice they do no such thing. See Chapter 1, footnotes 38 and 39, for example. There is a further contradiction for board members now, inasmuch as they have developed guidelines that standardize treatment in the name of fairness.

38. Amos, William, Member, U.S. Board of Parole, "The Parole Decision-Making Project of the U.S. Board of Parole," Address presented at the American Congress of Correction, Miami, August 1971, U.S. Department of Justice, *Parole Decision-Making: A Progress Report*, 61-62.

39. Evjen, Victor, "Current Thinking on Parole Prediction Tables," *Crime and Delinquency*, Vol. 8, No. 3, July 1962, 216-238; Hoffman, P. and Goldstein, H., *Do Experience Tables Matter?* Parole Decision-Making: Supplemental Report Four, National Council on Crime and Delinquency, June 1973.

40. See, for example, Gottfredson, D. et al., *Parole Decision-Making:*

Summary, National Council on Crime and Delinquency, June 1973, 6-8, 28, 46-57; Wilkins, L., *Parole Decision-Making, Report No. 6*, 28-29, 31.

41. Hayner, Norman, "Why Do Parole Boards Lag in the Use of Prediction Scores?" in R. Carter and L. Wilkins, eds., *Probation and Parole*, New York: John Wiley & Sons, 1970, 627; Clinard, Marshall, "Prediction of Recidivism," *Review of Sociology*, New York: John Wiley & Sons, 1957, 484-488.

42. Martinson, R. et al., "A Critique of Research in Parole," in Carter and Wilkins, *Probation*, 643-649; Robison, J., and Takagi, P., "The Parole Violator as an Organization Reject," in Carter and Wilkins, *Probation*, 233-254.

43. Robison, J., and Takagi, P., "The Parole Violator," 235; Department of Corrections, State of California, "Narcotic Treatment-Control Project—Phases I and II: A Synopsis of Research Report No. 19," May 1963.

44. Von Hirsch, Andrew, "Prediction of Criminal Conduct and Preventive Confinement of Convicted Persons," *Buffalo Law Review*, Spring 1972, 717-758,

45. Gottfredson, D., "The Base Expectancy Approach," in N. Johnston et al., eds., *The Sociology of Punishment and Correction*, New York: John Wiley & Sons, 1970, 807-813; Wenk, E., and Robison, J., "Assaultive Experience and Assaultive Potential," unpublished paper, Davis, California: National Council on Crime and Delinquency Research Center, May 1971. For an attempt at predicting suicide among mental patients, which illustrates this problem, see Rosen, A., "Detection of Suicidal Patients: An Example of some Limitations in the Prediction of Infrequent Events," *Journal of Consulting Psychology*, Vol. 18, 1954, 397. Rosen identified 30 of the 40 actual suicides, but incorrectly identified 2,990 nonsuicidal patients as suicidal.

46. In sum, ". . . items used in predictive studies have been mechanistic and restricted to experience before institutionalization, and to a large extent have given a static rather than dynamic picture of the ongoing process of adjustment to social norms and interpersonal relations in society" (Clinard, Marshall, "Prediction," 488).

47. Gottfredson, D. et al., "Summarizing Experience for Parole Decision-Making," *Parole Decision-Making, Report No. 5*, National Council on Crime and Delinquency, 1972, 40.

48. U.S. Department of Justice, *Parole Decision-Making: A Progress Report*, 4.

49. Ibid., 47.

50. Conrad, John, "Decisions," 71-72.

51. See cases cited earlier in Chapters 2 and 3.

52. U.S. Board of Parole, *Rules and Regulations*, 1974, Section 2.13.

53. Dawson, R., "The Decision to Grant or Deny Parole," 243-303.

54. It is futile to think the board could ever "get to know" an inmate under

the present system, with the tremendous case loads and short times allotted for parole hearings.

55. This is also questionable in light of previous discussion of rehabilitation behind walls.

56. U.S. Board of Parole, *Biennial Report*, 1968-70, 22.

57. See Table 3-2, Chapter 3.

58. Appendix 3A contains three examples of inmates whose case records indicate that they were refused parole because of the "seriousness" of their offense, regardless of any rehabilitative factors, any features of their parole plan, any excellent institutional performance, or any prognosis score for successful parole.

59. Sellin, T., and Wolfgang, M., *The Measurement of Delinquency*, New York: John Wiley & Sons, 1964.

60. Ibid., 237.

61. Ibid., 237-240. Totally ignored is the issue of power. Their analysis is abstract and completely isolated from the reality of structural conditions. Which people's judgments in fact determine what crimes will be considered serious?

62. These researchers had a rather naive and inadequate conceptualization of the power relationships in advanced capitalist society. The much maligned "middle class" does not have the power to define and organize the machinery of the legal and political system. See Mills, C.W., *White Collar*, New York: Oxford, 1951; Domhoff, W., *Who Rules America?* Englewood Cliffs, New Jersey: Prentice-Hall, 1967.

63. For a discussion of "ideological hegemony" see Hoare, Q., and Smith, G., eds., *Selections from the Prison Notebooks of Antonio Gramsci*, New York: International Publishers, 1972; Cammett, J., *Antonio Gramsci and the Origins of Italian Communism*, Stanford, 1967; Boggs, Carl, "Gramsci's Prison Notebooks," *Socialist Revolution*, Vol. 2, Nos. 5 and 6, September-December 1972, 79-118; 29-56.

64. Akman, D. et al., "The Measurement of Delinquency in Canada," *The Journal of Criminal Law, Criminology and Police Science*, Vol. 58, September 1967, 330-337; Normandeau, A., "The Measurement of Delinquency in Montreal," *The Journal of Criminal Law, Criminology and Police Science*, Vol. 57, June 1966, 172-177; Velez-Diaz, A., and Megargee, E., "An Investigation of Differences in Value Judgments between Youthful Offenders and Non-offenders in Puerto Rico," *J. of Crim. Law, Criminology and Police Science*, Vol. 61, December 1970, 549-553.

65. Rossi, P. et al., "The Seriousness of Crimes: Normative Structure and Individual Differences," *American Sociological Review*, Vol. 39, No. 2, April 1974, 224-237.

66. For an understanding of "conflict" theory, see Horton, John, "Order vs. Conflict Theories of Social Problems as Competing Ideologies," *American Journal of Sociology*, Vol. LXXI, No. 6, May 1966.

67. By presenting an already compiled list, taken from the Uniform Crime Reports where the FBI crime index is reported, the researchers limited the available choices as to what activities are considered crimes. Acts that are very harmful to our society, such as war, imperialism, racism, sexism, were not even presented as possible choices. Since white-collar crimes, which are injurious to people, are performed by the very persons who form the elite, it is not surprising that they are not considered very serious. It would appear that concessions are being made today in the area of "victimless" crimes, to give the appearance of movement towards real change.

68. Rossi, P. et al., "The Seriousness of Crimes," 231.

69. National Council on Crime and Delinquency, "The Practical Application of a Severity Scale," *Parole Decision-Making: Supplemental Report Thirteen*, June 1973, i.

70. See testimony and statement of Charlotte Reese, in *Hearings before Subcommittee No. 3*, 411-436, 744-758.

71. Robison, J., and Smith, G., "The Effectiveness of Correctional Programs," *Crime and Delinquency*, January 1971, 70-71; Babst, D. et al., "Relationship of Time Served to Parole Outcome for Different Classifications of Burglars . . ." National Council on Crime and Delinquency, 1969.

72. U.S. Board of Parole, *Biennial Report*, July 1968 to June 1970, 13.

73. Ibid., 22, 23.

74. Joseph Scott analyzed the relationship between various factors considered by the parole board and the amount of time imprisoned. He found that the seriousness of the crime was the factor best related to the severity of the punishment. ". . . parole board decision-making appears to be based almost exclusively on one . . . criterion, the seriousness of the crime, rather than on an inmate's institutional adjustment or . . . socio-biographical characteristics." Scott, Joseph, "The Use of Discretion in Determining the Severity of Punishment . . . ," *Journal of Criminal Law and Criminology*, 65, 1974, 214-224.

75. Hoffman, P., and Gottfredson, D., "Paroling Policy Guidelines," *Parole Decision-Making: Report No. 9*, National Council on Crime and Delinquency, June 1973, 10.

76. Ibid., 10-12.

77. Ibid., 10-12.

78. Ibid., 5.

79. Endicott, William, "State Parole: Gates Open to New Ideas," *Los Angeles Times*, May 8, 1975, 1.

80. Ibid., 24.

81. Mills, C.W., "The Powerless People: The Role of the Intellectual in Society," *Politics*, Vol. 1, April 1944, 72.

82. Quoted in Quinney, R., "With Some Notes on the Rise and Fall of American Criminology," *The Insurgent Sociologist*, Vol. IV, No. 1, Fall 1973, 63.

83. For further discussion of this issue, see Platt, A., and Cooper, L., *Policing America*, Englewood Cliffs, New Jersey: Prentice-Hall; and Center for Research on Criminal Justice, *The Iron Fist and the Velvet Glove*, Berkeley, 1975.

84. Mills, C.W., "The Powerless People," 70.

85. Mills, C.W., "The Contribution of Sociology to Studies of Industrial Relations," *Berkeley Journal of Sociology*, Vol. XV, 1970, 11-32.

86. Becker, H., "Whose Side Are We On?" *Social Problems*, Vol. 14, No. 3, 1972, 239-247.

87. Gottfredson et al., "Summarizing Experience," 6.

88. Ibid., ii, 18.

89. Ibid., 8. Note the attention directed to the relationship between military activity and activity in crime control, mediated by "science."

90. Ibid., 16-17; 29.

91. Ibid., 28.

92. Ibid., 43.

93. For an excellent analysis of the organization of work, see Braverman, Harry, *Labor and Monopoly Capital*, New York: Monthly Review, 1974.

94. Ibid., 47-52.

95. Wilkins, Leslie, "Some Philosophical Issues, Values and the Parole Decision," Foreword, *Parole Decision-Making, Report No. 9*, xi-xiii.

96. Ibid., xvi.

97. Gottfredson, D. et al., "Summarizing Experience," 62-63.

98. Ibid., 63.

99. See Horton, John, "Order vs. Conflict Theories of Social Problems as Competing Ideologies," *American Journal of Sociology*, Vol. LXXI, No. 6, May 1966, for a discussion of this and an alternative perspective.

100. Gottfredson, D. et al., "Summarizing Experience," 58. This is essentially correct. Inmates have no great love for the indeterminate sentence and the frustrations it produces. They would prefer a known fixed sentence with an end to the power of parole boards to prolong their time served for arbitrary and illogical reasons. However, this does not mean that inmates desire punishment as opposed to real efforts to help them find a place in the social world. Of course, the social world must be such that this becomes a possible reality. (See *The Outlaw, Journal of the Prisoners Union*, Vol. 4, No. 3, June-July 1975.)

101. Horowitz, David, "Social Science or Ideology," *Berkeley Journal of Sociology*, Vol. XV, 1970, 1-10.

102. A 1971 study conducted by the Research Division of the Department of Corrections showed that the selection of courses in vocational training programs at the California Institute for Women was based on their practical

contribution to the ongoing operation of the institution rather than an assessment of either the potential employee or the labor market (Mares, Renee, "La Pinta: The Myth of Rehabilitation," *La Gente*, March 1974, 6).

103. Perhaps threats of behavior modification experiments, maintaining some potential of earlier parole, just plain force (no work, no food, TV, recreation, school, etc.), or simple boredom will be used.

104. Mitford, Jessica, *Kind and Unusual Punishment*, New York: Random House, 1974, 210.

105. Ibid., 215.

106. The California Department of Corrections' 1970-71 budget report indicated that over a four-year period 1,071 prisoners on work furlough earned $840,000, of which about half was appropriated by the state. Men on work furlough must buy their own clothing, are not entitled to receive the $68 "gate money" upon release, must pay the prison for "room and board," and are compelled to provide their own transportation to and from work. (Ibid., 231.)

107. Jackson, George, *Soledad Brother*, New York: Bantam, 1970, 35, 37.

Chapter 5
Summary and Conclusions: The Fate of Parole

1. State Bar of California, Committee on Criminal Justice, *Report and Recommendations on Sentencing and Prison Reform*, June 1975, 1.

2. Fairbanks, Robert, "State High Court Lets Fixed-Term Prison Plan Die," *Los Angeles Times*, April 3, 1976, 1.

3. Studer, Robert, "Sentencing Bill Now Up to Brown," *San Diego Union*, September 20, 1976, 1.

4. *The Outlaw, Journal of the Prisoners Union*, Vol. 4, No. 3, June-July 1975, 1-4.

5. The committee defined *rehabilitation* to mean living in society without committing serious crimes.

6. A contradiction for liberals is that they see problems as arising from the social structure and then proceed to talk about changing individuals to fit in.

7. State Bar of California, *Report* 26.

8. Ibid., 26.

9. Ibid., 27.

10. Ibid., 34.

11. *The Outlaw*, 1-4.

12. O'Connor, James, *The Fiscal Crisis of the State*, New York: St. Martin's Press, 1973.

13. Rusche, Georg, and Kirchheimer, Otto, *Punishment and Social Structure*, New York: Columbia University Press, 1939.

14. Ibid., 5.

15. The term *mode of production* refers to the way in which existence is produced, life is maintained; it is the organization of relationships linking human labor to the environment. The mode of production consists of two elements: the forces and the relations of production. The *forces of production* are the instruments, tools, technological innovations, with which production is carried out. The *relations of production* are the social relationships among people engaged in the process of production. In a capitalist society, there is a *ruling class* that owns the means of production (forces) and the *working class* that has nothing but its labor power to sell. Between these two classes are smaller classes of people, the petty bourgeoisie and the managerial class. The *petty bourgeoisie* are principally small shopkeepers, small entrepreneurs, remnants from the early stages of competitive capitalism. The *managerial class* is that group of men who manage the corporations and industrial enterprises for the ruling class, who do not own the means of production, but are paid a salary for their labor power much in excess of the working class. (The class relationships under monopoly capital are still being debated. See, for example, Braverman, Harry, *Labor and Monopoly Capital*, New York: Monthly Review Press, 1974; Aronowitz, Stanley, *False Promises*, New York: McGraw-Hill, 1973.) Traditional sociologists tend only to deal with the forces of production, technology, industrialization, and to ignore the relations of production and the word capitalism itself. The term *material* refers to these fundamental, basic conditions of human existence. The materialist conception of social life and history is summed up in a paragraph Marx wrote in the Preface to *A Contribution to the Critique of Political Economy*:

In the social production which men carry on they enter into definite relations that are indispensable and independent of their will; these relations of production correspond to a definite stage of development of their material powers of production. The totality of these relations of production constitutes the economic structure of society—the real foundation, on which legal and political superstructures arise and to which definite forms of social consciousness correspond. The mode of production of material life determines the general character of the social, political and spiritual processes of life. It is not the consciousness of men that determines their being, but, on the contrary, their social being determines their consciousness (New York: International Publishers, 1970, 20-21).

16. Rusche, G., and Kirchheimer, O., *Punishment*, 19-23.

17. Ibid., 206.

18. Ibid., 137.

19. Were policy makers seriously interested in the welfare and humanity of

prisoners, they would institute real reforms, such as due process in prison hearings, adequate wages for work done, better work and educational opportunities, conjugal visits, and more humane general living conditions. Liberal criminologists and many social groups have suggested these things for years.

20. Weber, Max, *The Protestant Ethic and the Spirit of Capitalism*, New York: Scribner's, 1958, 181-182.

Index

Index

171

About the Author

Janet Schmidt received the Ph.D. from the University of California, Los Angeles, in March 1976, and is currently teaching criminology and the sociology of deviant behavior in the Department of Sociology, San Diego State University. Now also a part-time law student, Dr. Schmidt's previous experience includes teaching various grade levels from elementary to university. She co-authored a book that discusses schooling in the United States entitled *Cracks in the Classroom Wall* with Professors Tom Robischon and Jerome Rabow of UCLA, and is presently working on a text for classroom use in courses on criminology, deviant behavior, and social problems.